Robert Michu

Colour illustration by
Karolina Hołda

Messerschmitt
Bf 109F

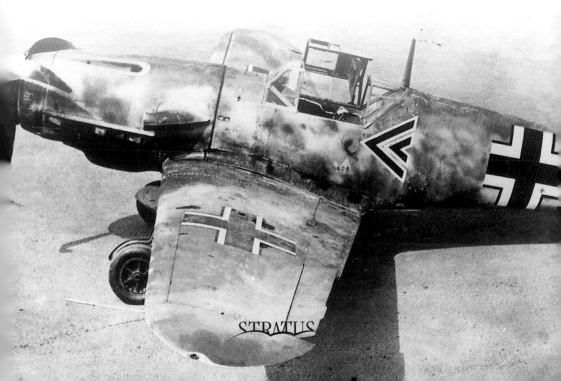

STRATUS

STRATUS s.c.
Po. Box 123,
27-600 Sandomierz 1, Poland
e-mail: office@mmpbooks.biz
for
Mushroom Model Publications,
3 Gloucester Close, Petersfield,
Hampshire GU32 3AX, UK.
E-mail: rogerw@mmpbooks.biz
© 2013 MMPBooks.
http://www.mmpbooks.biz

ISBN
978-83-61421-75-7

Editor in chief
Roger Wallsgrove

Editorial Team
Bartłomiej Belcarz
Artur Juszczak
James Kightly
Robert Pęczkowski

DTP
Stratus s.c

Colour Drawings
Karolina Hołda

Scale Plans
Dariusz Karnas

3D drawings
Dariusz Grzywacz

Printed by:
Drukarnia Diecezjalna,
ul. Żeromskiego 4,
27-600 Sandomierz
tel. (15) 832 31 92;
PRINTED IN POLAND

Table of contents

Acknowledgements 2
Early stages 3
Two programmes 6
Armament 9
Bf 109F-0 9
Variants 12
Series production 21
Modifications 26
Final variants 43
Research programmes 45
Production numbers 48
Technical Description of The Messerschmitt Bf 109F-2 49
Specifications 52
Colour Profiles 52
Detail Photos 78
General View 78
Fuselage 80
Engine 87
Wing 98
Canopy 103
Cockpit 106
Tail 112
Undercarriage 116
Armament 123

Acknowledgements

Although the writing process in itself is solitary work, many people have contributed photographs and information. Marek Kruk, Dénes Bernád, Marian Krzyżan, B. Barbas, (Flugzeug Publikations, GmbH), M. Griehl.

The author and the publisher would like to thank Major (Retired) Don Allen for providing colour photos.

Title page: Famous photo of the Bf 109F-2, W.Nr. 12764 from HQ I./JG 26 the pilot of which, Hauptmann Pingel, became a British PoW in July 1941 following a forced landing in Britain. A triangle with the C3 code, indicating the 96-octane petrol for the DB 601N engine, and thus the F-2 variant, can be seen clearly under the cockpit near the fuel filler. (Author's coll.)

Early stages

The history of the Messerschmitt Bf 109 was destined from the outset to be connected with Daimler-Benz engines, but due to industrial-design problems, a powerplant from that manufacturer was not fitted to the Messerschmitt fighter until 1938. The first variant of the engine, designated the DB 601A, was matched with the then latest Bf 109 version to make the Bf 109E, one of the best fighters in the world at the time. Despite this, the effects achieved were not satisfactory in all respects, mainly due to the hasty creation of the Bf 109E, nicknamed '*Emil*', after the DB 601A-1 was put into series production. For this reason, extensive work continued in parallel on a variant of the Bf 109 powered by the DB 601E engine, intended to be the ultimate standard fighter for the *Luftwaffe*. It soon turned out that an entirely different profile of the forward fuselage would be the chief characteristic feature of the new version. The change was made not only because of the compromise cowling on the Bf 109E, but because the DB 601E was 452 mm (17.79 inch) longer than the DB 601A. Additionally, an entirely new spinner was introduced for the new generation of Messerschmitt fighters and '*Zerstörers*' (twin engined heavy fighters, literally 'destroyers'), resulting from a change to the engine cooling system. Thanks to the lengthened nose and the use of the huge spinner, all the protrusions so typical of the '*Emil*', could be dispensed with. Cowling panels on the Bf 109F (nicknamed '*Friedrich*') were formed in such way that they provided good aerodynamics combined with exemplary ergonomics, facilitating servicing.

Along with the change of aerodynamics around the nose section of the new Bf 109, the tail of the aeroplane was redesigned, introducing a new, cantilever tailplane. A slight error was, however, made during calculations, which resulted in the fuselage-tail joint on the last, ninth, frame being too delicate for stresses imparted by the new, more powerful engine; this later necessitated the use of four external reinforcement bars. This solution

Two photos of the fourth Bf 109F prototype taken at the Messerschmitt factory at Augsburg in 1939. It is apparent that the new engine and its cowling were fitted on the fuselage of a Bf 109 D. Note the non-standard engine cowling immediately aft of the propeller, which seems to suggest an annular radiator, and also the split flaps, which suggest the earliest version of the new radiators were fitted in the modified wings. (MT via M. Krzyżan)

proved so simple and successful that it was not changed until the end of summer 1941 when, with the introduction of the Bf 109G in mind, the fuselage-tail joint was reinforced inside the skin. (This in response to the G-model's even heavier and more powerful engine). As the Bf 109G did not enter production according to the planned timetable, the modification proved instead to be a recognition feature of the middle-production series of the Bf 109F. (Later production Bf 109Fs saw the return of the external reinforcement bars).

As soon as the early research period was completed, in early winter 1938, assembly of the first two experimental prototypes (*Versuch*) for the Messerschmitt variant now called the Bf 109F commenced. The first of these, the Bf 109 V22, made its maiden flight on 26 January 1939, flown by the Augsburg plant test pilot, H. Beauvais. Its twin, the Bf 109 V23, was first flown soon afterwards. Both experimental machines were used to complete the initial research process for the 'Friedrich'. They were used for testing the engine, forward fuselage profile, new cooling systems and modified wings. The aircraft were known under the following designations:

Bf 109F V24 W.Nr. 1929 was used for engine trials and had airframe similar to F-1 version.

Aeroplane	Serial no.	Registration	*Stammkenzeichen*
Bf 109 V22	W.Nr. 1800	D-IRRQ	CE+BO
Bf 109 V23	W.Nr. 1801	D-ISHN	CE+BP

As opposed to the V22/V23, made to 'Friedrich' standards with improved fuselage and wings, the next two prototypes were intended for testing of alternative solutions.

This was a further pair of experimental aircraft:

Aeroplane	Serial no.	Registration
Bf 109 V24	W.Nr. 1929	?
Bf 109 V25	W.Nr. 1930	D–IVKC.

Both machines were fitted with the same, new, wings with elliptical tips, but the arrangement of the engine compartment differed. The V24/25 probably featured a non-standard oil cooling system, based on a frontal annular oil cooler (as with the Jumo 211 engines in the Junkers Ju 88), which led to the removal of the standard oil cooler under the engine, where the oil tank was probably housed. The cowling of the annular cooler overlapped the rear portion of the spinner, which on both prototypes had a new form, similar to that of the Me 210.

At the beginning the latter two aircraft were probably not considered to be 'Friedrich' prototypes, but instead were seen as experimental machines to test new design solutions. It was only later that they were included in the programme as prototypes, with new wings added. As opposed to the first pair of prototypes built from the outset as such, both these aircraft were experimental machines converted from two production Bf 109D 'Doras'.

It seems that, at least initially, there were no major differences between the Bf 109 V22 and V23. Later on, however, at the end of the development work, the Bf 109 V23, as the first full prototype Bf 109F, was fitted

The converted second prototype Bf 109F, probably in spring/summer 1940. The front engine cowling newly fitted aft of the spinner can be clearly seen, as can the very shallow oil cooler fairing under the engine and the new tail of the aircraft. Note also the wing tip, matching neither the modified wing nor the rounded wing tip standard (no navigation light). (MT via M. Krzyżan)

with the DB 601E engine, while its twin was still powered with the DB 601A. Both were used for research work on the aircraft, the power plant and its altered systems in the redesigned engine compartment. Progress was not impressive, due to engineering problems with the DB 601E engine, political problems due to the outbreak of war (which required concentration on mass-production of the Bf 109E), and the industrial limitations that forced the Germans to ration raw materials and funds for research work. All this led to the decision that the Bf 109F should initially be powered with the DB 601N engine, which was designed for 96-octane petrol and had been introduced into series production in early 1940 and, as of early August, installed also in the Bf 109E and the Bf 110D and E.

Willy Messerschmitt and one of the early Bf 109F. (AMC)

Two programmes

Due to separate research programmes conducted in parallel by Messerschmitt AG, the entire process of developing the Bf 109F should be seen as being divided into two main projects. The first was limited to modifying the standard-planform '*Emil*' wing with a general update of the design and entirely new radiators, and to redesign the fuselage to fit the new DB 601E engine. These were the initial features planned for the new variant of the Bf 109. The second stage came later and involved a modified wing planform, achieved by lengthening the span with elliptical wingtips.

The first project focused on one of the most important innovations used in the wings of the new Bf 109; the fitting of a completely new type of radiators in the wings. In their final form the radiators were twice as wide and half as deep as those in the Bf 109E, but at the same time they featured a novel design solution; this comprised a special two-piece (top and bottom) airflow flap aft of the radiator, in place of the single-piece item as used in '*Emils*'. In this design the bottom flap not only adjusted the airflow, but also acted as the landing flap.

It seems the new radiators were first used at an early stage of the modified wing development. The earliest available data mentions them as early as the summer of 1939. This is indicated in a letter from the LC 2/RLM department of 2 August, which announced that a new, light radiator had been developed by DVL, and an experimental Bf 109 was required to enable a testing programme to be carried out. Such an aeroplane, in the form of the Bf 109E W.Nr. 1256, became available in January 1940, after the initial research process for the radiators was completed. The DVL radiators were subsequently installed, the process taking until 20 May, whereupon the aircraft performed 35 hours of test flying with just one failure. Meanwhile, another 109 was allocated for tests of the competing SKF radiator, which was fitted during April of that year and subsequently tested. The radiator from that company proved superior and was later fitted in production aircraft.

As regards the engine, it was a more powerful variant of the DB 601, intended to give the aircraft a higher speed. The first generation of the engine (A/B) was to be a standard version for universal use, while the next generation (DB 601 E/F) was developed from the outset to be fitted in newer, more modern and faster aircraft versions (the Bf 109F and the Me 210) and thus to phase out the first generation. In both cases the engine was planned to be fuelled by 87-octane petrol.

A series of shots of the Bf 109F-0, W.Nr. 5604, VK+AB in August 1940. The aircraft already has the deeper oil cooler and standard carburettor air intake, but the wings are still in the initially modified version. This is what the production Bf 109F would have looked like had its production commenced as planned, in the spring of 1940. (Author's coll.)

The design work on the DB 601E engine was plagued with problems and probably constituted the main cause of delays in engineering work on the Bf 109F. At an early stage the problems forced the designers to use the DB 601N ('*Nordpol*') as an alternative power plant. The main difference between the DB 601E and the DB 601N lay in the power output: the DB 601E produced 1,350 hp (1,007 kW) at 2,700 rpm, which was 175 hp (130 kW) more than the DB 601N could develop 1,175 hp (876 kW) at 2,600 rpm. This was paid for by a slight loss of operational altitude, as the E engine attained its maximum output at lower altitude (4,800 m) (15,748 ft), than the tuned N type (5,200 m) (17,060 ft).

After production lines for the DB 601E were started in early 1940, only a handful were manufactured, and not enough to build up the reserve required for mass production of the new fighters. For example, of the 79 DB 601A and E engines that had been assembled on one of the lines by May 1940, only a dozen or so were Es. The situation with the N was hardly better: only 40 DB 601Ns were assembled during that period. Thus, there were only enough DB 601Es for factory and state trials, and only enough DB 601Ns for preparation of the first delivery to the aircraft manufacturer. In comparison, Daimler-Benz engine factories had produced 7,699 standard DB 601As over that time.

The second stage of the work that led to the F variant was to introduce new wings with elliptical tips. Their structure was altered, though still based on the basic design already used in the modified wing. Slat, aileron, and flap dimensions were altered, for example, in order to improve or maintain their operating characteristics. The new wing with the rounded tip was added to the '*Friedrich*' program in the summer of 1940; production was started about the same time as the F-0 batch of pre-production aircraft in August, and this, needless to say, caused another delay in the Bf 109F trial program.

One of the main changes compared to the Bf 109E: the new radiators fitted deep inside the modified wings, which also constituted a part of the landing flaps. Here they are shown probably in the prototype version ('Adler').

One of the most characteristic features of the Bf 109F: cowlings opened in three ways offering free access to the entire engine. (G. Petrov)

One of the first Bf 109F-1s built at the WNF plant during late 1940/early 1941, W.Nr. 6631, PH+BE. The square-shaped air intake was the tell-tale feature of Bf 109Fs from this factory at the time. The close-up view shows clearly the air intake and the nose profile characteristic for the successors of the Bf 109E. (Author's coll.)

Armament

The armament of the new Messerschmitt version was another matter. The Bf 109E had been developed from the outset as the successor of the Jumo 210-engined Bf 109, and it shared the earlier aircraft's armament layout where some of the guns were placed in the wings. The '*Emil*'s' successor was to be an aircraft with all guns (including cannon) in the fuselage, this layout having been fought for by design offices for years. This was not straightforward, however, since the principal aircraft cannon of the *Luftwaffe* (MG/FF) could not be used in this way. The 15 mm MG151/15 heavy machine gun would prove better, having been designed from the outset to be fitted in the fuselage and fire through the propeller boss, but it had not been developed to sufficient maturity by 1940. Production of the Bf 109F without this gun made little sense. Therefore, regardless of the wing modification and engine problems, the Germans had to wait until the main armament was made reliable for Bf 109F production to start.

The same aircraft in a demonstration flight over the Alps, showing the beauty of the Bf 109F to advantage. The photos were taken for a Messerschmitt advertisement. (Author's coll.)

Bf 109F-0

After the first test stage was completed successfully, the Messerschmitt company signed an agreement with the RLM to build a trial batch of the Bf 109F in form of fifteen Bf 109F-0s; this was to be completed between November 1939 and about April 1940. The first aircraft were without a doubt intended to act as prototypes for the production model, and then to allow the manufacturer to eliminate any shortcomings that arose during service use.

After only three aeroplanes were assembled during January 1940, the entire 'Friedrich' programme was halted, probably at *Reichsmarschall* Hermann Göring's orders, to limit any experimental work. Production was stopped even though the WNF factory, which closely co-operated with Messerschmitt in the programme, had already made preparations for series production of the Bf 109F. By April 1940, sub-assemblies had been produced there and assembly of the first fuselage, wing and tail for the Bf 109 F-1 was under way, the first flight being originally scheduled for July. This deadline was soon changed, so that according to the *Lieferplan* 17 the first five production 'Friedrichs' of the 720 ordered from that factory, would not be ready before October. Eventually this deadline was not met, probably due to the introduction of new wings in the Bf 109F programme.

This Bf 109F-0, W.Nr. 5604, VK+AB, was used to test the improved engine installation.
(Flugzeug Publikations, GmbH)

About the end of May 1940, probably as a result of the strong likelihood of victory over France, it was decided to revive the '*Friedrich*' programme, and thus to resume production of the Bf 109F-0, albeit to a slightly different configuration than the three aircraft produced at the beginning of the year. The first of these was assembled in late June, and 14 F-0s had been built by February 1941. Then in March, another one was assembled, two more in May and the last one in June. Altogether 19 Bf 109F–0s were built between June 1940 and June 1941, as planned.

Aircraft of the F-0 version differed from aircraft to aircraft, in some cases quite significantly. This was due to constant improvements being introduced. For example, the first five Bf 109F-0s featured the modified wings and it took some time before some of these received the wings with rounded tips. All these aircraft were fitted with DB 601A (W.Nr. 5601, 5604 [VK+AB] and 5605) or DB 601N (W.Nr. 5603) engines. Of the nine prototype and pre-production aircraft produced by mid-July 1940, the DB 601E engine had been fitted to only one aeroplane, the Bf 109 V24, in which this powerplant replaced a DB 601A. It took more time before some of the prototype and subsequent pre-production machines also received the DB 601E. The aircraft W.Nr. 5605, VK+AC, was the first of these, later probably re-designated the Bf 109 V26 and in March 1941, together with the Bf 109F-1 (W.Nr. 5643, D-IGUD) included in the DB 601Q engine research programme. The trials ended in partial success and, in June 1941, the WNF factory started assembling a batch of 24 DB 601Q-powered Bf 109F-4/Us. Due to persistent problems with these engines, however, the programme was abandoned by early July of that year and the aircraft were reconverted to standard F-4 specification.

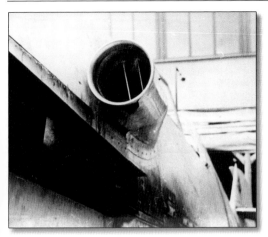

This and opposite page:
Seven different supercharger air intakes
as tested on Messerschmitts with the
Bf 109F in mind. Three more intakes
are known, one of which can be seen
in the earlier photo of the Bf 109 V23,
W.Nr. 1801, CE+BP.
(MT via M. Krzyżan)

Variants

Following negotiations with the RLM, the Messerschmitt company offered production of the 'Friedrich' in several variants. In common with the Bf 109 'Emil', a 'heavy' version (MG FF/M 20 mm cannon in the fuselage) and 'light' version (MG151/15 15 mm machine gun in the fuselage) would be produced. However, due to problems with the DB 601E engine, it was decided to develop four models:

F-1 – 'heavy' version with the 'temporary' DB 601N engine;

F-2 – 'light' version with the 'temporary' DB 601N engine;

F-3 – 'heavy' version with the DB 601E engine, successor of the F-1;

F-4 – 'light' version with the DB 601E engine, successor of the F-2.

Initially, in the spring of 1940, the Erla and WNF plants also planned to build reconnaissance versions based on all 'Friedrich' models, but due to excessive demand for fighters this idea was abandoned, and the gap was filled by the reconnaissance 'Emil'. It is worth noting that the RLM attached a surprisingly great importance to the reconnaissance version. For example, no fewer than 145 reconnaissance F-1 machines out of the total of 255, and 305 reconnaissance F-3s out of 465 on order were requested from the WNF!

The price of a Bf 109 in the F-1/F-2 version was set at RM90,000 with a manufacturing run of about 250 aircraft (so it was less expensive than the 'Emil', which cost the same per aircraft when a run of 550 machines was made), and the price of the F-3/F-4 was set at RM70,000 with a planned production of just over 450. With the order increased to 830 Bf 109Fs at the end of 1941, an average Bf 109F price tag was less than RM56,000. Such a low unit price when compared to the 'Emil' resulted mainly from continuous simplification of Bf 109 production technology. While constructing an 'Emil' initially took almost 20,000 man-hours, which fell to less than 9,000 by the last batches, the assembly of an early series 'Friedrich' took just over 16,000 man-hours, and less than 7,000 for aircraft made in the final batches.

Final preparations for series 'Friedrich' production commenced in August 1940. It was then that the Bf 109F-0, W.Nr. 5602, was fitted with the new wing and, probably, the DB 601E engine, and sent for trials as

The first production Bf 109F-1.
(Flugzeug Publikations, GmbH)

the prototype Bf 109F-4. At the same time the Bf 109F-0, W.Nr. 5604, VK+AB (fitted with a DB 601A engine) became the pattern for series production of the Bf 109F in general and it went to Rechlin for state trials in August 1940. The Bf 109F-1 was selected as the first version to be put in series production, with the Bf 109F-0, W.Nr. 5603 (fitted with a DB 601N engine) as its prototype, undergoing tests at Rechlin until about mid-July. The priority of the F-1 was not denoted by the '1' in its designation – it was dictated simply by the lack of DB 601E engines required for F-3 and F-4 variants, while production of the MG151/15 required for the F-2 was only just beginning. At the same time (July 1940), Bf 109F-0 W.Nr. 5605 was used in tests of the mounts for this new armament that had been produced by Ikaria and Messerschmitt. The Bf 109F-1 would be something of a transition version, manufactured in small numbers, in order to deliver initial aircraft to units for introduction, and to give factories time to gain experience and practice in their production.

Bf 109F of Oberst. *Mölders, this time an F-2 flown by the ace from February 1941 and into the spring of that year. (MT via M. Krzyżan)*

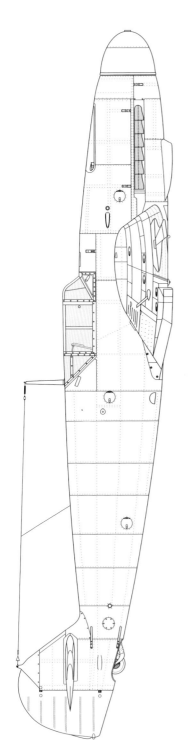

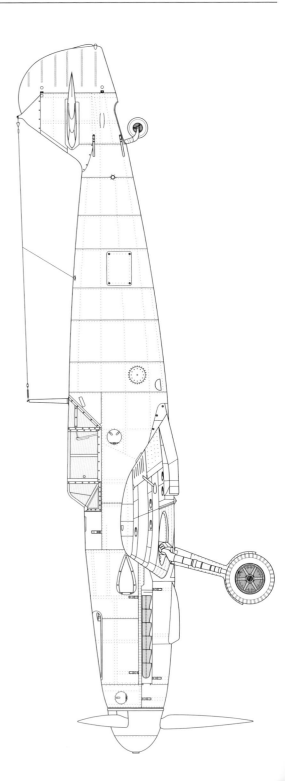

Bf 109F-1 side views. 1/48 scale.

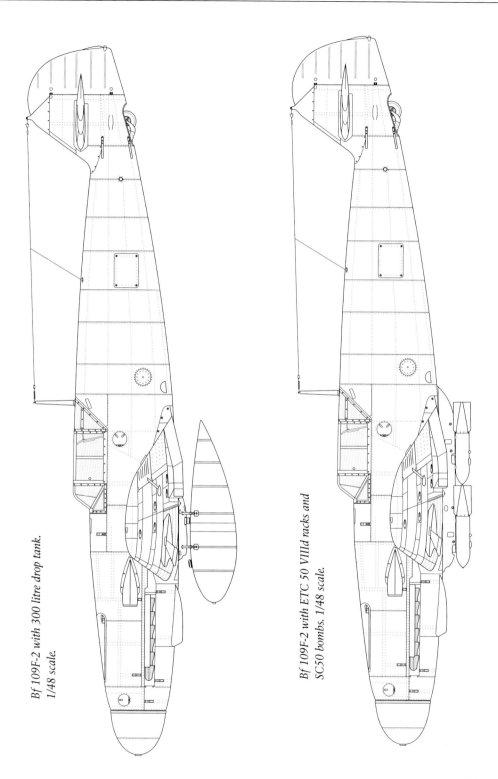

Bf 109F-2 with 300 litre drop tank.
1/48 scale.

Bf 109F-2 with ETC 50 VIIId racks and
SC50 bombs. 1/48 scale.

3D drawing of the Bf 109F-1 nose produced by WNF factory.

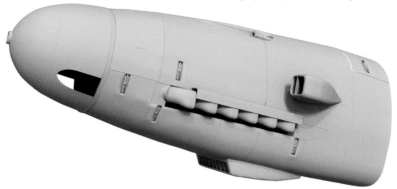

3D drawing of the Bf 109F-4 nose.

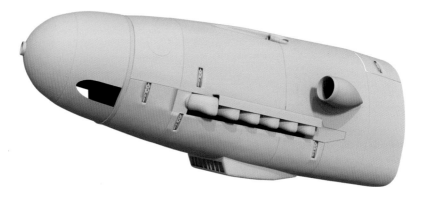

3D drawing of the Bf 109F-4/Z nose. Note deeper oil cooler under the fuselage.

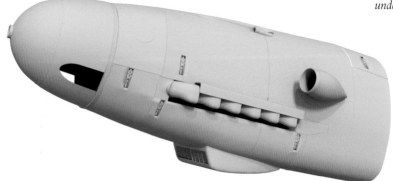

All drawings D. Grzywacz

Above and left: One of the earliest
Bf 109Fs with JG 51, flown at the
end of 1940 by another great ace
of the Luftwaffe, Oberst *Werner
Mölders.* This is Bf 109F-1, W.Nr.
5628, SG+GW, which had already
been flown on operations by the
JG 51 commander in early October
1940. (B. Barbas)

Bf 109F-2 from I./JG 51 (probably 2. Staffel)
at an airfield in northern France, spring
1941.(MT via M. Krzyżan)

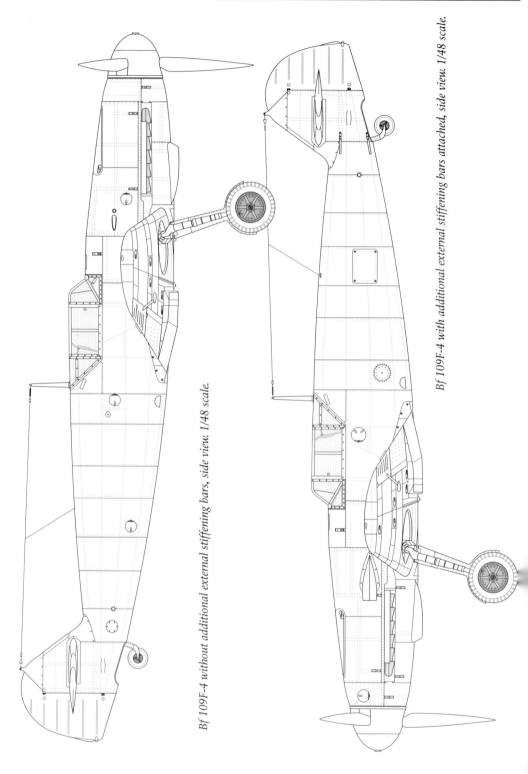

Bf 109F-4 without additional external stiffening bars, side view. 1/48 scale.

Bf 109F-4 with additional external stiffening bars attached, side view. 1/48 scale.

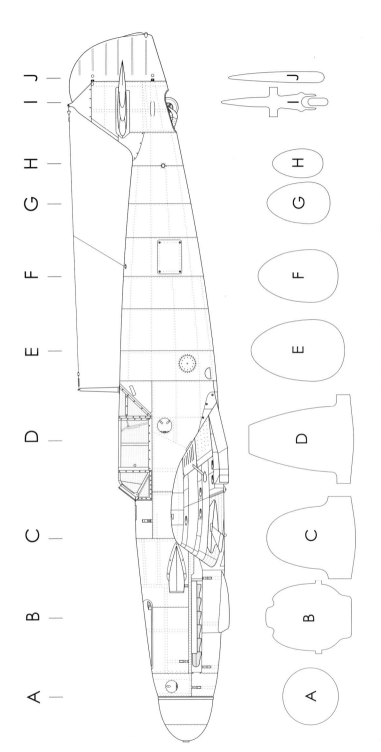

Bf 109F-4 fuselage cross-sections. 1/48 scale.

Bf 109F-4 front (above) and rear (below) views. 1/48 scale.

Series production

After successful trials at Rechlin, the '*Friedrich-1*' was put into series production, starting around the end of September, at the Messerschmitt factory in Regensburg. In October, as the first batches of MG 151/15 heavy machine guns started to be delivered, production of the Bf 109F-2 also commenced there. In November, assembly of this model commenced at AGO, and of the F-1 at the WNF plant. By the spring of 1941 the Messerschmitt plants at Regensburg and Augsburg had assembled a total of 157 aircraft, comprising 19 F-0s and 138 F-1s (with each F-0 naturally taking much longer to complete than the production machines). Over almost the same period (November 1940 – January 1941) the WNF plant delivered 49 F-1s (out of 50 planned), and then began assembly of the F-2. As opposed to other '*Friedrich–1s*', all the first F-1 batch assembled at the WNF and the first F-2s had distinctive angular air intakes. Even though no Bf 109F-1 production was planned for the summer of 1941, Messerschmitt factories continued to turn them out due to other delays. The last two '*Friedrich-1s*' were assembled in June and July, bringing the number of aircraft of this variant to 206.

Although by the spring of 1941 a total of 226 Bf 109Fs had been built (out of 610 planned), the aircraft failed to play an important part in operations at this time. The low numbers, allowing the formation of just one fighter wing, were undoubtedly a problem, but most of all the numerous shortcomings in the early '*Friedrichs*' prevented extensive use of the type. These difficulties involved the oil and charging systems, which made the aircraft difficult to operate and unreliable. Therefore their operational use during that period was scarce.

Another reason behind this situation was the season, when bad weather made it impossible to test-fly completed aircraft and deliver them to units. Such a situation had its advantages, however. Thanks to the standstill, a programme of extensive front-line trials was completed, which detected the main causes of the '*Friedrich*'s' problems and permitted them to be resolved at the factories. As a result, aircraft of the later F-2 series, and subsequently the F-4s, displayed excellent flying and operating characteristics.

Production of the Bf 109F-3 was started in October 1940 by Messerschmitt factories at Regensburg and, perhaps, by WNF at Vienna. This was the least successful variant of the '*Friedrich*' and it was assembled in minimal numbers, probably only to keep the factories working. It seems probable that all the machines of this variant, a mere 15 in total, were later converted to other versions. There is an unusual case to quote as an exam-

Bf 109F-2 of III./JG 54 at Pleskau (Pskov) airfield.
(Flugzeug Publikations, GmbH)

ple here: Bf 109F-3, W.Nr. 5004 lost at Fuka in Africa on 10 July 1942 by 4.(H)/12. This would have been an F-3 fighter converted to a reconnaissance version.

In January and February 1941 respectively, two more factories started making the F-2 (in fact the first machines were completed in the last days of December 1940), which was built until September that year as the basic 'Friedrich' variant. Then in May 1941 the first F-4s started to leave the assembly lines, and their production continued until the middle of the following year.

The aircraft differed between them with regard to the engine and armament: the F-2 featured the DB 601N and MG151/15, while the F-4 was powered by the DB 601E, and armed with the new MG151/20. This new weapon proved virtually perfect for its time. As opposed to the similar-calibre

Bf 109F-2 of I./JG 51. (Flugzeug Publikations, GmbH)

MG FF/M, this 20 mm cannon featured a long barrel and a more advanced, much more reliable design. It wa belt- rather than drum-fed, and it offered the excellent rate of fire of 800 rounds per minute, with high muzzl velocity. Experience proved it was effective not only against aerial targets, but also against light armoured vehicle:

Bf 109F-2, W.Nr. 9704 flown by Oberstleutnant *Günther Lützow. Photo was taken after his 101st victory on 24 October 1941. (Flugzeug Publikations, GmbH)*

Above: Bf 109F-4 of JG 51. (Flugzeug Publikations, GmbH)

Below: Early Bf 109F-4 flown by Major *Werner Mölders as* Kommodore *of JG 51. (Flugzeug Publikations, GmbH)*

Bf 109Fs of II./JG 52.

Right: *Bf 109F-4 of 8./JG 5 based at Petsamo.*

Bottom: *Bf 109F-4 of III./JG 52 at the airfield during ferry flight. (All photos Flugzeug Publikations, GmbH)*

Two photos of a Bf 109F-4 of 7./JG 52 parked in front of the hangar at a Russian airfield.
(Flugzeug Publikations, GmbH)

Modifications

Tropical Variants

The Bf 109F-4 had a tropical sub-variant designated the F-4/*trop*. Externally, the '*trop*' could be distinguished from other Bf 109F-4s by the tropical filter on the supercharger air intake, and also by the cockpit sunshade attachments. The prototype Bf 109F-4/*trop*, which also included a number of other minor modifications, was first flown in late June or early July 1941, and then in August its production commenced hastily at Erla. The haste was due to a large demand for the tropicalised fighters in connection with operations in the USSR and Africa. Once the news spread around the *Luftwaffe* that a tropical version of the Bf 109 had been developed, the RLM was barraged with requests from units to equip them with these aircraft, or to supply filter kits to be fitted by unit repair workshops. For example, in mid-June requests for the filters were received from *Luftflotte* 2 and for F-4/*trop* aircraft from II./JG 54 fighting at Leningrad. A month later filters for Messerschmitts were requested by the HQs of *Luftflotte* 5 (for 20 Bf 109T's) and *Luftflotte* 4 (for a total of 320 kits). The RLM persistently rejected these requests, in part because by June only 220 filter kits were available, and in any case these were only for '*Emils*', which could not be fitted at unit level. By the end of July 1941 only 60 tropical kits for the '*Friedrich-4*' were ready, while the demand for Bf 109F/*trop* aircraft was estimated at 680 machines.

Some documents suggest the existence of a tropical reconnaissance version of the '*Friedrich-2*'. For example the OKL list of losses shows at least one F-2 loss from a reconnaissance unit operating in Africa in 1942. It is highly probable that these aircraft were converted and modified rather than built in that form, but it is not certain if this affected large numbers of F-2 machines, or just a few.

Bf 109F-4/trop of I./JG 27, 1942. Aircraft maintenance on a frontline airfield. (Flugzeug Publikations, GmbH)

Above: Bf 109F-2/trop, 'White 2' of JG 27 in North Africa.

Right: Bf 109F, 'Yellow 5' of 9./JG 27 destroyed near Gazala, spring 1942. Tropical filter is clearly visible.

Bottom: Bf 109F-4/trop, 'Yellow 14' of 3./JG 27 usually flown by Lt Hans-Joachim Marseille. (all photos Flugzeug Publikations, GmbH)

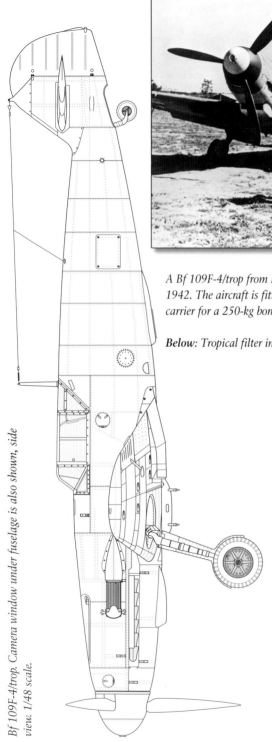

A Bf 109F-4/trop from I./JG 3 during operations in the Mediterranean in 1942. The aircraft is fitted with armoured glass and an under-fuselage carrier for a 250-kg bomb. (CAW)

Below: Tropical filter in open position. (D. Grzywacz)

Bf 109F-4/trop. Camera window under fuselage is also shown, side view. 1/48 scale.

Opposite page: Two shots of a Bf 109F-4/Z/trop with the GM-1 system fitted, showing factory code of PK+XH, during a demonstration flight, 1941. An identical aircraft can be seen in the background, but with markings of II Gruppe (probably JG 27). Note the changed shape of the main wheel wells: as opposed to the first Bf 109Fs, which were originally planned to have covered wheels, production Bf 109Fs were soon seen with round wells, shaped to enclose the wheel tightly. (IWM)

GM 1

Another version of the Bf 109F was the sub-variant fitted with the GM 1 temporary engine boost system. roduction of Bf 109F-2s so equipped commenced in the spring of 1941 at the WNF factory, and of '*Friedrich*-4s' ith the system in the autumn of that year. These aircraft were known as the F-4/Z, or F-4/Z/*trop* when tropical- ed. Subsequently, production was expanded at Erla, which apparently saw the assembly of over 1,200 F-4/Zs. n the '*Friedrich*-4s' this solution made it possible to increase the top speed by about 20 km/h at an altitude of ghtly above 6,000 m, which allowed the aircraft, in turn, to achieve marked superiority over every enemy fighter, cluding the Spitfire Mk V, which was at the time the principal adversary of German pilots. Aircraft of this version atured a larger oil cooler, the Fö 870, the same type that later became standard in the '*Gustav*'. Interestingly, as

pposed to the '*Emil*- 'Z' or '*Theodor*-1/Z' ghters, the F-4/Zs d not have their GM tanks in the fuse- ge, but in the wings, mediately aft of the heel wells, with one nk in each wing. loreover, these were sually not the typi- l cylinders, as used earlier versions, but rcular tanks.

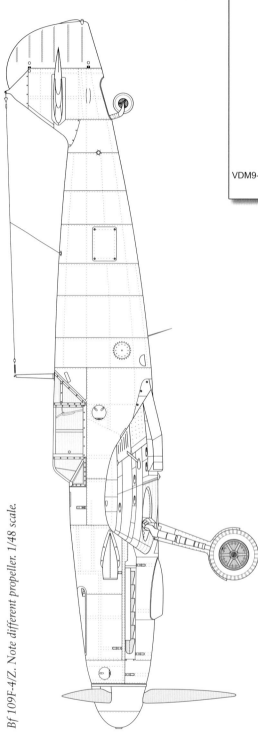

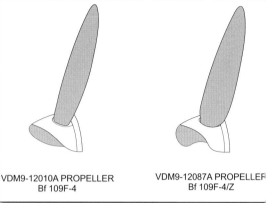

VDM9-12010A PROPELLER
Bf 109F-4

VDM9-12087A PROPELLEF
Bf 109F-4/Z

Other changes

Apart from the above mentioned sub-variant
the F-version aircraft featured certain differenc
between individual batches and models. The first
these was the introduction of a modified, stiffene
and reinforced, tail that enabled the removal of th
external reinforcement bars. This change affecte
the later F-2 series. In the F-4 the reinforcemen
bars featured in the earliest and last batches. Thes
were, respectively, the batches that appeared in sprir
and early summer 1941, and those assembled i
late 1941 by Erla in the case of the F-4/*trop* an
F-4/Z/*trop*, and in service in spring and summe
1942. The fact that such late-series aircraft reverte
to the external reinforcement bars resulted from
the conversion of earlier Bf 109F-1/F-2/F-3 aircra
to F-4 standard, probably due to long delays in th
Bf 109G programme.

Another alteration took place in the spring c
1941, when the angular carburettor air intakes we
finally abandoned in the Bf 109Fs made by WN
This was connected with the introduction, as stanc
ard, of the more streamlined intake typical of th
Bf 109F-2 made by Messerschmitt. In the summe
it was changed to a more bulky unit, typical of th
Bf 109F-4, which could be fitted with dust filters.

The next alteration was to introduce a ne
propeller, as a result of which individual batche
of the F-2 and F-4 aircraft could be fitted with tw
different propellers – the VDM 9-12010A wit
narrow blades (mainly seen on F-2s) and the VDI
9-12087A with wider blades (mainly seen on F-4s

The latter propeller was fitted initially in aircraft that used the GM 1 system, but it later became a standard feature of the 'Friedrich-4'.

After the fighter was put into production, probably in the latter half of 1940, Messerschmitt designers developed a system of switches to cut off one part of the coolant system should one of the radiators be damaged. Thus, if the aeroplane was hit in one radiator, the pilot was able to isolate it from the cooling system and direct the coolant into the undamaged radiator under the other wing. This allowed the aircraft to continue flying, at a lower engine rating, and save the aeroplane. Unfortunately for the pilots, plants that manufactured the Bf 109 failed to introduce the device as a standard item in every aeroplane, but manufactured it separately and fitted it only in certain batches of aircraft. Some of these kits were sent to front-line units, where specialist ground personnel fitted them to aircraft already in service. It seems peculiar, in view of how potentially useful the system was, that the concept was abandoned once '*Friedrich*' production ended.

Rüstzatz

Another area of difference between aircraft was in the wide range of armament and equipment sets, the vast majority of these being factory-fitted, which meant that the new fighter was delivered to units in several different main variants. The F-4

A series of photos showing one of the rarest Bf 109F variants, the Bf 109F-4 with five-point armament, including two MG151/15 guns located in under-wing pods. The manufacturer assembled only 240 such machines, which were designated the Bf 109F-4/R1, and some of these, shown in these photos, were delivered to I./JG 52 in 1942. (B. Barbas)

saw a number of modification kits, either the *Rüstzatz* type, such as the R5 (an external tank rack), or th
Rüstzustand, such as the R1 (two MG151/15 guns in under-wing pods – only 240 machines were so modified

The latter category also included the R7 (probably two variants of bomb rack fittings, with ETC 500 IX
and ETC 50 VIIId racks, commonly designated with a letter, as the F-4/B); the R2, R3 and R4 (three differe
reconnaissance modifications, using different cameras and with the radio sets removed); R8 (another reconna

*Reconnaissance Bf 109F-4s from 1.(F)/122, which operated the tropicalised version of the Bf 109F from Sicily
in the summer of 1942. At the time the trop versions of 'Friedrichs', as well as 'Gustavs', already had special
cut-outs in the port side of the cockpit to allow the fitting of sunshades to protect pilots at readiness from direct
sunlight. The close-up shot of the cockpit shows the faired-over starboard side of the cockpit canopy with an
opening for the signal discharger, and the armoured glass panel on the windscreen. (NASM)*

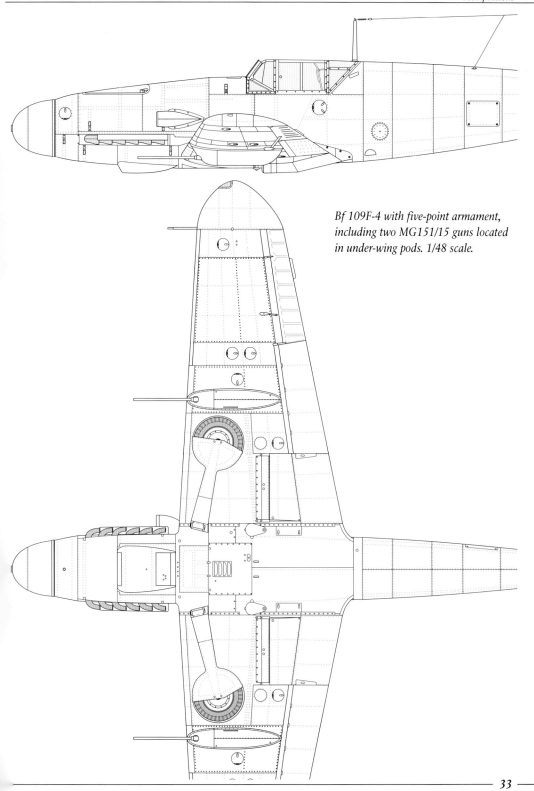

Bf 109F-4 with five-point armament, including two MG151/15 guns located in under-wing pods. 1/48 scale.

Above: A reconnaissance Bf 109F of unit operating in Western Europe in 1942. The fact that this is not a fighter is shown by the letter code and the special camouflage, partly resulting from the modification of the aircraft during its conversion from a fighter to a reconnaissance version (the wing leading edges are covered with a stripe of RLM 70 or similar colour). (Author's coll.)

Below: A reconnaissance Bf 109F taxies for take-off somewhere in the west in 1942. An external tank installation can be seen under the fuselage, and aft of it a fairing for a fuselage camera and FuG 25 IFF aerial. Some reconnaissance 'Friedrichs' had their armament removed. (Author's coll.)

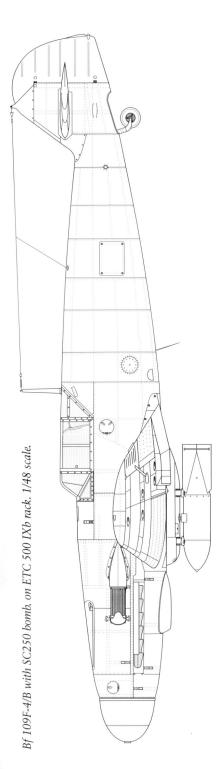

Bf 109F-4/B with SC250 bomb. on ETC 500 IXb rack. 1/48 scale.

sance version, this time with a radio set – officially 43 were built, but in fact many more existed, probably by conversion). These reconnaissance variants were introduced into service during late 1941/early 1942, after the demand from fighter units was met, and they were converted from the Bf 109F-4/Z. The R2 sub-variant was fitted with Rb 20x30 cameras, the R3 with Rb 50x30 cameras, the R4 with Rb 75x30 cameras, and the R8 with Rb 50x30 cameras.

The *Rüstzustand* category probably included a modification with two BSK 16 camera guns in the wings, adjacent to the wheel wells. This system was used in the Bf 109F-4 and probably also in the Bf 109F-2, which was subject to a number of modifications of this kind, but probably within a slightly different numbering system. There were certainly models with additional tanks (R5) or with two types of bomb racks (e.g. the F-2/B).

One of the most interesting modifications of the 'Friedrich-4' among those mentioned above was the R1, which was a scheme to arm the aircraft with two more 15 mm (.6 inch) MG151/15 guns in under-wing pods. This modification was evolved by replacing the 15 mm (.6 inch) guns with two 20 mm (.8 inch) MG151/20 cannon, of the type which formed the main armament of the Bf 109F-4 (as opposed to the Bf 109F-2). Work on this type of armament commenced no earlier than the autumn of 1941, and it was completed by the summer of the next year. Early in the spring of 1942, Bf 109F-4, W.Nr. 7449, which had been built at the WNF factory and earmarked for trials of the new armament, was sent to Tarnewitz. The first prototype kit of the cannon and pods themselves, designated V1, reached Tarnewitz by rail, as bad weather prevented their transport by air. The armament was fitted at the *E-Stelle* and ground tested; poor characteristics and malfunctioning were noted. In result, the entire system had to be dismantled, tested on the ground, and then re-fitted in the aeroplane with some modifications.

The first air firing trial was made on 24 March 1942, followed by 60 trials flights, after which the armament was found to be little better. The aeroplane was sent back to the manufacturer with a list of comments, and replaced in early May 1942 by the first trial batch, of four Bf 109F-4s prepared at the WNF factory. Trials of these machines were carried out in early May and comprised 27 flights. The port cannon failed 16 times, including six times prior to firing 100 rounds; the starboard cannon failed 17 times, including five times prior to firing 100 rounds. The aircraft were sent back to the manufacturer with comments, in order to introduce corrections in the preparations for series production of such machines, and with the instruction to modify the four test aircraft. During 11-16 May, four front-line aircraft were converted to the new standard and transferred to I./JG 52. There a special *Kommando* under *Lt.* Rüttger was set up and sent for tests to Tarnewitz, where the improved armament system was tested on the ground and, on one aircraft, in flight. The *E-Stelle* expressed reservations, and the section of Messerschmitts rejoined their *Gruppe* at the eastern front.

Soon afterwards tests of another 'Friedrich-4', W.Nr. 13149 (also from WNF production) were made, its under-wing armament being modified directly at Tarnewitz. The first three ground firings were satisfactory, but during the first three flights, on 28-30 May, the armament failed. The mechanisms were corrected and 12 more flights were flown, with just one failure taking place, while on two further occasions it was necessary to reload the cannon after it jammed.

As a result of all these trials and corrections, the under-wing armament was declared satisfactory – this did not mean specifically that it worked, but simply that it created no danger for the pilot. In other words, the MG151/20 cannon were the best solution among the available alternative armaments, and they were employed more out of necessity than as the best solution. This is clearly indicated by the overall conclusion of the tests carried out at the *E-Stelle* Tarnewitz, which stressed the unreliability of the armament and the impractical ammunition arrangement, as the rounds had to be placed very carefully, and it was safer to load just 100 rounds, rather than the planned 135.

Meanwhile, in another attempt to reinforce the Bf 109F's firepower it was planned to fit two 13 mm (.5 inch) machine guns above the engine. The aircraft thus armed was designated the F-4/U1, but this modification was soon abandoned. This was in fact a continuation of work that had been done on the F-2/U1, of which only one example had been produced to act as an experimental aeroplane, for armament trials. This machine was tested in combat conditions by Adolf Galland.

A sequence of photos that document what seems to have been the rarest models, with reinforced armament: the Bf 109F-2/U1 and the Bf 109F-6/U1 (specifically: W.Nr. 6750). The former is an aircraft with two 13 mm MG 131 above the engine, and the latter is a Messerschmitt with two 20 mm MG FF/M cannon in the wings. Both were flown in the spring of 1941 by A. Galland in JG 26. (B. Barbas)

Bottom: Note details of the horizontal stabiliser and landing flaps.

Another two photos of the Galland's Bf 109F-2/U1 with two 13 mm MG 131 above the engine clearly visible. (B. Barbas)

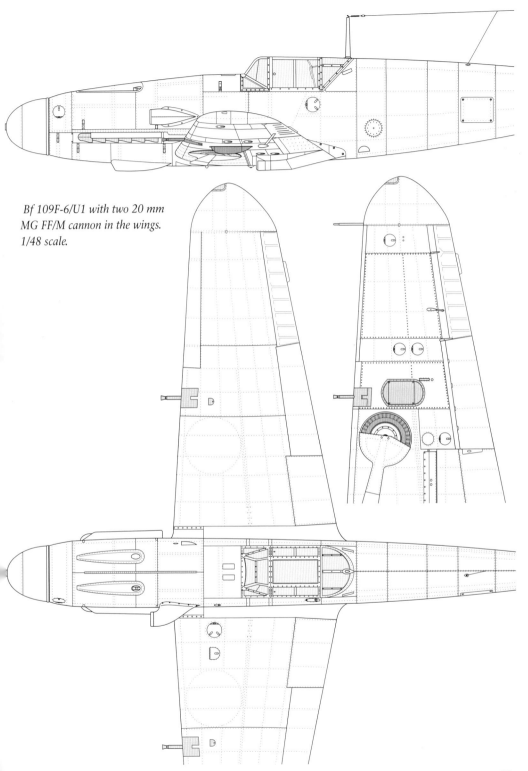

*Bf 109F-6/U1 with two 20 mm
MG FF/M cannon in the wings.
1/48 scale.*

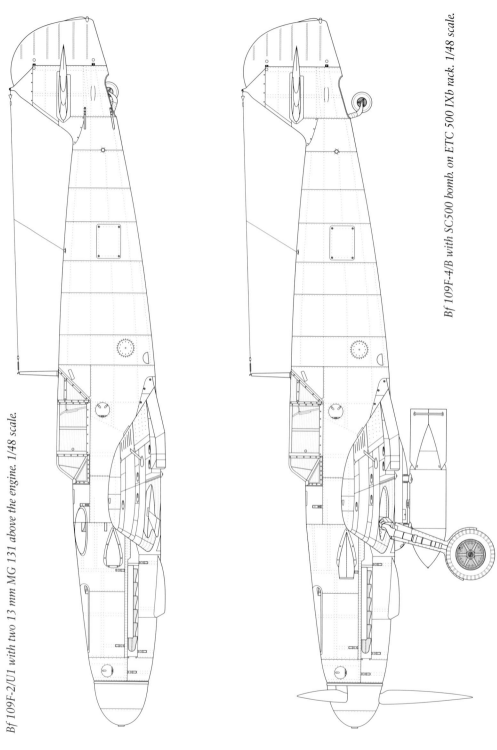

Bf 109F-4/B with SC500 bomb. on ETC 500 IXb rack. 1/48 scale.

Bf 109F-2/U1 with two 13 mm MG 131 above the engine. 1/48 scale.

Above: A Bf 109F-2 with a 250 kg (550 lb) bomb attached accelerates for action against Britain, as shown by the markings of the specialised Jabo flight of JG 26. Bomber versions of the F-2 and F-4 were seen in two broadly used variants, the C and D, able to carry a 250 kg (550 lb) bomb or four 50 kg (110 lb) bombs, respectively, both existing as variants of one Rüstzustand. (Author's coll.)

Below: Loading a Bf 109 with four 50 kg (110 lb) bombs with whistles, used against infantry by flights of JG 51, 52 and 54 on the Eastern Front. (CAW)

Above and below: Two photos documenting different schemes of winter camouflage in the same Wing, but in I Gruppe. The photos show two different Bf 109F variants: a Jabo *(with a 250 kg /550 lb bomb), and a pure fighter, lacking even the attachment for an external fuel tank. (M. Griehl)*

Bf 109F-4/trop from HQ III./JG 53 taxies for take-off in Africa in 1942. It can be seen clearly that the aircraft is fitted with outer armoured glass, and does not have the external fuel tank pylon. (MT via M. Krzyżan)

Final variants

Sometime in late summer or early autumn of 1940, at the time of the '*Friedrich*'s' introduction to the production lines, it was decided to develop versions with more powerful armament in the wings. All work on the programme was concentrated at the WNF plant, but controlled by the Messerschmitt office at Regensburg.

It seems that initially a whole range of new '*Friedrich*' models was considered, from F-5 to F-8. Available data shows that each of these was planned to be a development version of the F-1 to F-4 machines. It is difficult to find any concrete information regarding the F-7, but available sources suggest that it was intended to be the successor to the Bf 109F-3 which was, however, the greatest failure of all the '*Friedrich*s', and of which only a dozen or so examples were built. It seems that was the reason why the F-7 never existed in practice, remaining as a project only. The same fate overtook the F-5 – the intended successor to the '*Friedrich*-1' – which was assembled only in marginally higher numbers than the Bf 109F-3.

Thus only two versions remained among the proposed new sub-types, and in October 1940 the RLM placed large orders for these: no fewer than 1,281 of the Bf 109F-6 would be assembled and 1,112 of the Bf 109F-8. It is worth noting here that the decision as to which models should be selected was taken after prototype test results were known, as well as initial operational experience with the earliest Bf 109Fs. These must have proved beyond doubt that the central MG FF/M was a complete failure. Only the F-2 and F-4 armed with the MG151/15 were left, and these were used to develop the following variants:

Bf 109F-6 – successor to the '*Friedrich*-2' with the DB 601N engine, and armament consisting of two MG17s and a single MG151/15 in the fuselage plus two MG FF/M in the wings;

Bf 109F-8 – successor to the '*Friedrich*-4' with the DB 601E engine, and armament consisting of two MG17s and a single MG151/15 in the fuselage, plus two MG FF/M in the wings.

Meanwhile, in the autumn of 1940, production of the new MG151 cannon variant started to be prepared. The weapon was increased from 15 mm to 20 mm (.6 to .8 inch) calibre and in some, minor, respects it was improved compared to the original. This would seem to suggest that it was for this reason that the F-4 production was halted and the variant was rearmed with the MG151/20 cannon in place of the MG151/15 originally planned. As a result of this change there was a huge gap in production of the DB 601E-engined Bf 109F, almost

A Bf 109F-4/trop from late 1941 production batches. The reinforcement bars on the rearmost frame can be seen under the tailplane. These disappeared from new machines in late spring or early summer 1941, and then reappeared on some batches of the Bf 109F-4 at the end of 1941. (Author's coll.)

four months passing between the termination of the F-3 production and the start-up of F-4 production. During that time only one version of the 'light' fighter (F–2) was built.

The question of the new armament also paralysed the 'five-point' Bf 109F projects. The MG151/20 design proved so successful that it was intended to steadily, and as quickly as possible, phase out the MG FF/M cannon. In fact, by 1941 this weapon was categorised as temporary supplementary armament only. However, the MG151 cannon could not be squeezed into the wing, so had to be carried in special pods under the wings. In this context the entire programme of a Bf 109F with wing-mounted MG/FF armament was cancelled and when, in summer–autumn 1941, long-term tests of the '*Friedrich*' with MG FF/M cannon in the wings ended, construction of the under-wing pods became the main focus.

Several aircraft with wing-mounted armament were built. These were completed some time during late 1940 or early 1941 at the WNF factory, which closely cooperated with Messerschmitt AG. At least three prototypes for the F-5 and F-6 versions were built during this period, as well as a prototype for the Bf 109F with '*Messflügel*'. Work on the two prototype Bf 109F-5s continued at WNF as early as November 1940, which means that they were completed in December at the earliest. Considering the weather conditions in winter, it may be that the first flight took place as late as January 1941. One of the prototypes was based on one of the first Bf 109F-1s built in that factory (from the batch W.Nr. 6001-6010), while the other was probably never finished, or was immediately converted to another sub-variant.

The Bf 109F-6 was very similar to the '*Friedrich-5*', although it was in fact considered an alternative to the F-5 as it was based on a Bf 109F-2 (W.Nr. 6750) built in March 1941. Similar to the Bf 109F-5, the '*Friedrich-6*' featured more powerful armament in the wings, in the form of MG FF/M cannon; in this case, there is photographic evidence. The main difference between this and the F-5 was the fuselage armament: the F-5 received the MG FF/M cannon, while the F-6 was originally armed with the MG151/15, as it was developed from the F-2. However, in about the summer of 1941, its central cannon was replaced with the MG151/20, thus creating the Bf 109F-6/U. After a series of factory and state trials, the aeroplane, together with an Bf 109F-2/U1 (fuselage armament: one MG151/15 and two MG 131s) was delivered for front-line tests to *Stab./JG 26*, whose *Geschwaderkommodore Oberst* Adolf Galland had complained regularly about the weak armament of the '*Friedrich-2s*'.

The wing-mounted armament was fitted in the same portion of the wing as in the '*Emil*', immediately outboard of the main wheel wells. This was the same part of wing which was used in '*Friedrichs*' to fit camera guns and GM-1 cylinders. It is worth noting that in the case of the Bf 109F wing the cannon fit differed somewhat than in the '*Emil*-1'

Research programmes

Many Messerschmitt Bf 109Fs were used in research programmes, for new designs for future Bf 109s. Some of the most unusual tests were performed using two aircraft: one prototype and an aircraft selected from production machines. Both had their inboard wing sections redesigned and were fitted with a new type of main undercarriage, similar to that of the Me 209 project. Moreover, the first of these, the Bf 109 V23, W.Nr. 1801, CE+BP, was also fitted with a nose wheel on a long leg, thus making the first tricycle undercarriage on a Messerschmitt aircraft, as this was the layout intended for the Me 309. In the case of Bf 109F-1, W.Nr. 5642, SG+EK, renamed the Bf 109 V31, the main undercarriage was converted and a pressurised cockpit fitted, plus the entire engine cooling system was converted to bring it to the standard requested for the Me 209 and Me 309. (The radiators and oil cooler were fitted inside the fuselage in a special retractable structure). The Bf 109 V24 was another aeroplane allocated to the Me 309 programme, and it had its engine (the DB 605A in this case) cooling system converted completely, in a similar fashion to that of the *Versuch*-31, and was sent for wind tunnel tests at Göttingen and Chalais-Meudon.

Bf 109 V23, W.Nr. 1801, CE+BP used for testing Me 309 undercarriage layout. (Flugzeug Publikations, GmbH)

The Bf 109 V35, W.Nr. 9246, TH+TX was one of the most interesting prototypes based on production Bf 109Fs, as it was used during the spring of 1943 for a series of trials with RZ 65 air-to-air missile launchers fitted in the wings. The weapon dated back to the late 1920s/early 1930s, when the brilliant and enterprising designer, Reinhold Tiling, created a family of 65-100 mm missiles, which became the basis for *Wehrmacht* research from 1934, which in turn led to the RZ 65. Another stage of work on such a missile, aimed at developing the rocket into a practical weapon, was initiated in mid-1941 and finalised in the spring of 1943. The project proved a blind alley, though, and the *Luftwaffe* HQ decided to adapt army missiles instead. Initially the WGr. 210 rocket was utilised, following which in 1944, a new weapon was evolved in the form of the 55-88 mm (2-3.5 inch) R4M and '*Panzerblitz*'. These missiles resembled Tiling's designs of ten years earlier, not to mention the Soviet RS-82 and RS-132 missiles, which were also derived from Tiling's prototypes from before 1934.

A series of photos depicting one of the most interesting prototypes based on the Bf 109F: the Bf 109 V35, W.Nr. 9246, TH+TX, used in the spring of 1943 for testing of wings with built-in RZ 65 missile launchers. (MT via M. Krzyżan)

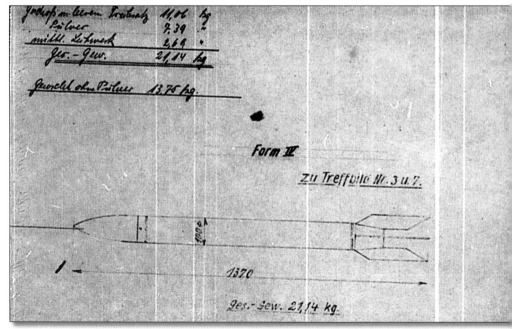

Bf 109F-2, W.Nr. 8195, VD+AJ assembled at Erla, was used for trials of a ski undercarriage and replaced a previously destroyed Bf 109E for winter tests. (M. Griehl)

The Bf 109F-2, W.Nr. 8195, VD+AJ, was used for repeated tests with ski landing gear, similar to those conducted in the winter of 1940-41 on a Bf 109E-8. That aeroplane crashed during its 87th flight, in the first half of February 1941 during resistance tests, and that was when the prototype '*Friedrich*' was substituted. The ski undercarriage, slightly different from that used in the '*Emil*', was not retractable due to its size and weight (the standard wheel wells were faired over).

During December 1941 an F-4, W.Nr. 7413 underwent a series of interesting comparison tests against an Fw 190A-2 at Rechlin. These trials proved the Bf 109 showed better acceleration, but the Focke Wulf proved as fast, or slightly faster (by about 10-20 km/h) (by about 6-12 mph) in level flight at sea level and at an altitude of 4,000-4,500 m (13,123-14,764 ft). The Fw 190 was faster in a dive but found it more difficult to recover, and was also slower in the climb than the Bf 109.

Several of the first Bf 109Fs were used as prototypes for its successor, the Bf 109G. The earliest trials were probably conducted on a F-0 batch '*Friedrich*' (W.Nr. 5604, VK+AB), and also on some experimental machines of the Bf 109F range (V25–V29). The new Bf 109 version initially did not differ from the Bf 109F at all in most respects. According to specifications, the engine would be the main difference; the DB 601E was planned to be replaced with the DB 605A which gave 125 hp (93 kW) more power but weighed 56 kg (123 lb) more at 756 kg (1,667 lb). While the DB 601E used 290 litres (64 gal) of fuel per flying hour at cruising speed at ground level, the DB 605 used 320 litres (70 gal), resulting in the range being reduced from 705 km (438 miles) for the Bf 109F to 630 km (391 miles) for the Bf 109G.

Final work on the DB 605A was beset with problems, though, and the first pre-production Bf 109G-0s (W.Nr. 14000 onwards), which had been assembled from October 1941, were fitted with the DB 601E instead. As a result, the new version of the Bf 109 initially differed externally from its predecessor only by its canopy. This was patterned on that of the Bf 109F, but converted to enable the cockpit to be pressurised. The Bf 109 V30 (W.Nr. 5716, ND+IE) and V30A (W.Nr. 5717, ND+IF) based on the Bf 109F–1 were prototypes for the G-1, the first variant of the Bf 109G. The Bf 109G also included many minor design changes, all of which it seems resulted from the Bf 109F's production development. In this respect, the Bf 109G could be regarded as a refined Bf 109F, in terms of production technology, fitted with a new engine.

Production numbers

The Bf 109F was built from October 1940 until June 1942. As a result, while the Bf 109E was the top *Luftwaffe* fighter for two wartime years, and the Bf 109G for three, the '*Friedrich*' dominated for just one year, 1941. Despite that, this model has often been considered the best variant of the Bf 109, with some justification. Putting aside the design shortcomings of the Bf 109 series, the Bf 109F combined the advantages of both the Bf 109E and the Bf 109G: lightness, speed, and manoeuvrability. This followed from the fact that the aircraft was well balanced and at the same time its aerodynamics were improved, a result of an accumulation of the design work conducted gradually by Messerschmitt since 1938. If the Bf 109E was a temporary version, compromised by the haste of its development, the Bf 109G, although derived from the Bf 109F, was over-burdened, due to the heavier engine and the changes in weight distribution it required, so it could not provide the pilot with such ease of handling as the Bf 109F enjoyed.

Exact numbers of the Bf 109F built are not certain, but it is known that by June 1942, when the Bf 109G appeared on the production lines, some 3,300 '*Friedrich*' had been assembled. Since the production effort largely focused on the F-2 and F-4, the number included some 1,840 '*Friedrich*–4s' and some 1,380 '*Friedrich*–2s'. It has to be remembered, though, that according to the aircraft production organisation in the Third Reich, some of these aircraft were converted and reintroduced into service as new ones. It is known, for example, that only about 50 Bf 109F-1s were assembled, but there is no confirmation that this many aircraft were delivered to units, which might suggest that they were later converted to the F-2 or F-4 standard. This was certainly with the case with the F-3, of which 15 were probably assembled, and then in part converted to other versions.

Bf 109F known W.Nr. serial blocks (*not all numbers were allocated*)

Bf 109F-0	Bf 109F-1	Bf 109F-2	Bf 109F-3	Bf 109F-4	Bf 109F-5	Bf 109F-6
5601 5602 5603 5604 5605 5606 5607 5608 5609 5610 5611 5612 all (MR)	5601 – 5760 (MR) 6601 – 6650 (WNF)	5401 – 5560 (Ar) 5601 – 5750 (MR) 5960 – 5990 (WNF) 6651 – 6850 (WNF) 7010 – 7150 8071 – 8330 (Erla) 8901 – 9000 (MR) 9151 – 9350 (MR) 9531 – 10000 (Ar) 12601 – 13000 (AGO)	None Known	7001 – 7660 (WNF) 8261 – 8900 (Erla) 10001 – 10300 (Erla) 13001 – 13390 (WNF)	8754 15556	None Known

(Ar) – Arado Rostock
(MR) – Messerschmitt Ragensburg
(WNF) – WNF Wiener Neustadt
(Erla) – Erla Leipzig
(Ar) – Arado Rostock
(AGO) – AGO Magdeburg

Technical Description of
The Messerschmitt Bf 109F-2

The Bf 109F-2 was a single-engine, low-wing, cantilever monoplane of all-metal construction, with retractable undercarriage.

The wing was of all-metal two-piece, single-spar construction, tapered, with rounded tips, and fitted with automatic leading edge slats. Each wing was attached to the fuselage by three points. The stressed skin was made of flush-riveted aluminium panels.

Ailerons were of metal construction, fabric covered, mass balanced, and actuated by push-rods. Slotted flaps were of metal construction, but fabric covered, operated by a large knob on the port side of the cockpit. Two-part screens to control the air flow in the under-wing radiators worked together with the flaps. Navigation lights were installed at the wing tips.

The fuselage was of duralumin, semi-monocoque construction, and was oval in cross-section. The forward section included the cockpit, which was enclosed by a two-part canopy, and the fuel tank. The central section was riveted onto the rear section, which was made of two halves joined in the vertical plane. Each half was made up of eight segments. Each segment ended with a Z-profile frame with oval cut-outs for stiffening stringers. Each half was stiffened with five stringers. The tail support, which formed the end of the fuselage, was attached by bolts to the rear section. The tail wheel well, and the jack and locking mechanism for the tail wheel, were located in the lower fuselage. The stressed skin on the fuselage was formed of flush-riveted aluminium panels.

The tail support attachment was additionally reinforced with external stiffening bars, which were attached by screws onto the support and the last segment of the fuselage.

The cockpit was partially armoured: the pilot was protected from the back and below by three armour plates attached by screws to the floor and the frame between the cockpit and the fuel tank.

A Bf 109F-4/trop from one of the late-1941 production batches. Note the cockpit: internal components can be seen clearly, including an internal armour glass panel, and the faired over starboard forward corner of the canopy. (Author's coll.)

The windscreen of the three-piece canopy was often complemented by additional screw-on armour glass in a steel frame. Small triangular windows were located at the bottom of the windscreen, the starboard one usually screened, and the signal discharger port was located there. The forward side window of the canopy could slide open. Two 6 mm (.2 inch) armour plates (rear and upper) were used, attached to the opening section of the hood. This section of the hood opened to starboard, together with the armour attached to it. It could be jettisoned in emergency, together with the rear section and the aerial mast.

An additional armour plate was located in the fuselage immediately aft of the fuel tank.

The tail was of all-metal construction. The tailplane was cantilever, tapered with rounded tips, metal-covered, with a fabric-covered elevator. The tailplane was adjustable in flight within + 1° 10' and –6', using a knob on the port side of the cockpit. The elevator was both horn – and aerodynamically-balanced.

The vertical tail surfaces had an asymmetric aerofoil to balance the propeller torque. The fin was metal-covered, the rudder fabric-covered. The elevator was both mass – and aerodynamically-balanced.

Elevators were actuated by push-rods, and the rudder by cables.

Undercarriage – conventional layout with tail wheel. The main undercarriage legs attached to both sides of the fuselage and retracted into wells, half-covered with single-piece covers, located in the wing undersides. The undercarriage featured hydraulic actuation, with an optional emergency lowering capability. The legs were VDM items with oleo shock-absorbers. Wheels had recessed profile hubs and 650×150 mm (26x6 inch) tyres, and were fitted with drum-type hydraulic brakes. Wheel track was 2.10 m (6.8 ft).

The 290×110 mm (11x4 inch) tail wheel was fitted in a fork, attached to its leg with an oleo shock-absorber, and was partly retractable in flight.

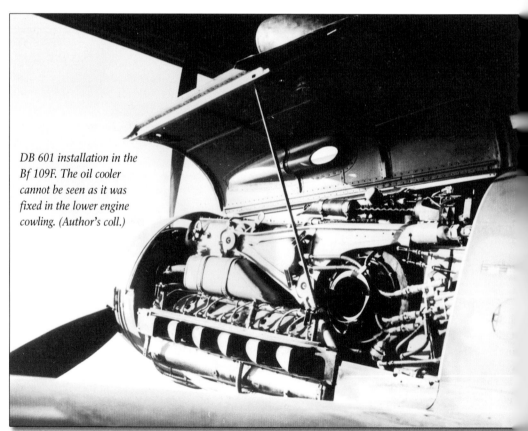

DB 601 installation in the Bf 109F. The oil cooler cannot be seen as it was fixed in the lower engine cowling. (Author's coll.)

The engine was a 12-cylinder in line, inverted-V, liquid-cooled Daimler-Benz DB 601N, rated at 864 kW (1,175 hp) at 2,600 rpm at sea level. The engine drove a 3.0 m (9.8 ft) three-blade all-metal VDM 9-11207A propeller. The engine was cooled with a 50:50 mixture of water and ethylene glycol, with the addition of 1.5% of *Schutzol* 39 rust preventive agent, circulating in a closed circuit. The cooling system included two equalising tanks on both sides of the engine, and two radiators beneath the wings, aft of the main spar. Air flow through the radiators was controlled by flaps in the lower part of the intakes, actuated by hydraulic jacks controlled automatically with thermostats, and two large outlet flaps along the wing trailing edge.

Fuel system – the main fuel tank was a self-sealing 400-litre (88 gal) unit made of soft plastic. A small tank with a manual injection pump located in the floor was used for priming the cold engine with light petrol fractions. The manual injection pump was located on the port side of the cockpit.

The aircraft could be fitted to take an additional 300 litre (66 gal) under-fuselage drop tank, connected to feed the main tank.

The engine pump was supported by an electric pump fitted in the main tank. A system of filters with cut-off valves was fitted forward of the fireproof bulkhead. The fuel used was 96-octane C3-type.

Oil system – this consisted of a 56.5 litre (12 gal) semi-circular metal tank (only 50.0 litres /11 gal of oil were used, leaving the rest of the tank empty for expansion). The tank was located around the main reduction gear at the front of the engine, and the oil cooler was located at the bottom of the engine cowling, and the gear pump with the oil thrower. Air flow through the cooler was controlled by a hydraulically-operated flap, adjusted automatically by a thermostat. Intava-Rotring or equivalent oil was used.

An hydraulic system served to raise and lower the undercarriage and to adjust the radiator and oil cooler flaps. Also the main wheel brakes were hydraulic, but that was an autonomous circuit, not connected with the main system. The movement of the liquid was forced by a 12 l/min. (3 gal/min) pump driven by the aircraft engine. The system included a 2.3 litre (0.5 gal) equalising tank fitted on the port side of the fuselage mount.

The aircraft's oxygen system was based around three two-litre cylinders in the fuselage aft of the cockpit. The filler valve was located on the starboard side of the fuselage. The pressure in the cylinder set filled completely was 1.5 MPa. Oxygen was fed to the pilot's gear located on the floor near the starboard side of the cockpit. The breathing mixture was fed up to an altitude of 8,000 m (26,247 ft), and at altitudes in excess of 8,000 m (26,247 ft) pure oxygen was provided.

The electric system had a nominal voltage of 24 V. Bosch 500 – 2,000 W generator was driven by the aircraft engine. A 7.5 A/hr battery was located in the rear fuselage (the 6th segment of the fuselage). All electric circuits were protected with automatic fuses.

The standard armament of the Bf 109F-2 consisted of two synchronised 7.92 mm (.3 inch) Rheinmetall-Borsig MG17 machine guns with 500 rounds per gun (on StL 17/1 mounts) and a 15 mm Mauser MG151/15 heavy machine gun with 150 rounds, fitted in the MoL 151/1 mount. The gun was belt-fed from a box in the port wing. The container for spent cases and links was located under the cockpit floor. External weapons consisting of bombs and additional 15 mm (.6 inch) guns were also used. The MG17 guns were cocked by a pneumatic system, and the MG151 by an electric system. Two cylinders for the pneumatic system were fitted in the rear fuselage at the battery shelf.

Equipment: the Bf 109F-2 was equipped with a full set of navigation and flight control instruments, and engine controls as required for single-engine fighter aircraft. A Walther signal discharger was located on the starboard side, beneath the windscreen, to fire signal flares. Moreover, all aircraft were fitted with a first-aid kit in the compartment on the port side of the fifth segment of the rear fuselage) and food in the rear fuselage. It was possible to fit the aircraft with a single-man dinghy located in the pilot's seat recess.

The radio system consisted of a FuG VIIa radio set, and some aircraft also featured the FuG 25 IFF. The FuG VIIa radio included two separate sets: the S5b transmitter/E5a receiver, powered by a U4 b/24 converter.

Specifications

	Bf 109E-4	Bf 109F-2	Bf 109F-4/trop	Bf 109G-2
Span (m)	9.87	9.92	9.92	9.92
(ft)	32.3	32.5	32.5	32.5
Length (m)	8.64	9.02	9.02	9.03
(ft)	28.3	29.5	29.5	29.5
Height (m)	2.6	2.6	2.6	2.50
(ft)	8.5	8.5	8.5	8.5
Wing area (m^2)	16	16.1	16.1	16.1
(ft^2)	172.2	173.3	173.3	173.3
Useful load (kg)	2,073	2,135	2,150	2,250
(lb)	4,570	4,707	4,740	4,960
Take-off weight* (kg)	2,656*	2,652	2,667	2,759
(lb)	5,855	5,847	5,880	6,082
Take-off/fuel** (kg)	3,141	3,137	3,152	3,244
	6,925	6,916	6,949	7,152
Engine	DB 601A	DB 601N	DB 601E	DB 605A
Range*** (km)	520	600	580	550
(mi)	323	373	360	342
Altitude (km)	10.3	11.2	12	12
(ft)	33,800	36,750	39,400	39,400
Speed at sea level (km/h)	460	495	538	525
(mph)	286	308	334	326
at 3,000 m (9900 ft)	520	–	557	583
(mph)	326	–	346	362
Max. speed/altitude	550/5,800	595/5,200	624/6,500	642/6,000
(mph at ft)	342/19,000	370/17,000	387/21,000	399/19,700
Cruise (km/h)	480	–	534	590
(mph)	298	–	332	337
Climb rate (m/min)	18	20.5	22.1	21
	59	67	72,5	69

* including armour but without armoured glass in the windscreen
** conventionally for all, rounded up to 485 kg: weight of the fuel, external tank and system
*** operational, that is at operational ceiling and combat engine output

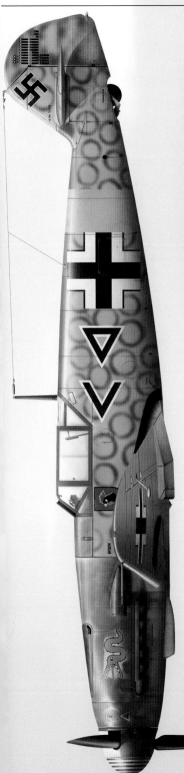

Bf 109F-2, W.Nr. 5458, personal aircraft of Hptm. Hans von Hahn, Kommandeur of 1./JG 3, July 1941 The Stab markings on this aircraft are unusual. Standard Luftwaffe camouflage of RLM 74, RLM 75 and RLM 76. The fuselage camouflage consisted of remarkably regular rings, either in RLM 74 or, more likely RLM 70, over RLM 76. The RLM 25 Tatzelwurm of Stab 1./JG 3 appears on the engine cowling and green and white circles on the spinner tip. The cowling and rudder have been oversprayed to tone down the bright yellow identification colours. The victory bars represent 24 aerial victories plus three aircraft destroyed on the ground and three balloons. Note also the area of dark, heat-resistant paint applied over the wing root to protect the fuselage from exhaust staining.

Bf 109F-4, W.Nr. 7183 of Stab III./JG 2, France, July 1941. One of the machines flown by Hptm. Hans 'Assi' Hahn and later decorated with victory bars on the rudder. Finished in an RLM 74/75/76 scheme, and carried the Stab markings of the Kommandeur of III./JG 2 The emblem of the 'Richthofen' Geschwader and personal emblem are visible. Gruppe vertical bar as most frequently seen on Stab aircraft. The white Stab markings were also a feature of JG 2's aircraft. Heat-resistant paint applied over the wing root to protect the fuselage from exhaust staining.

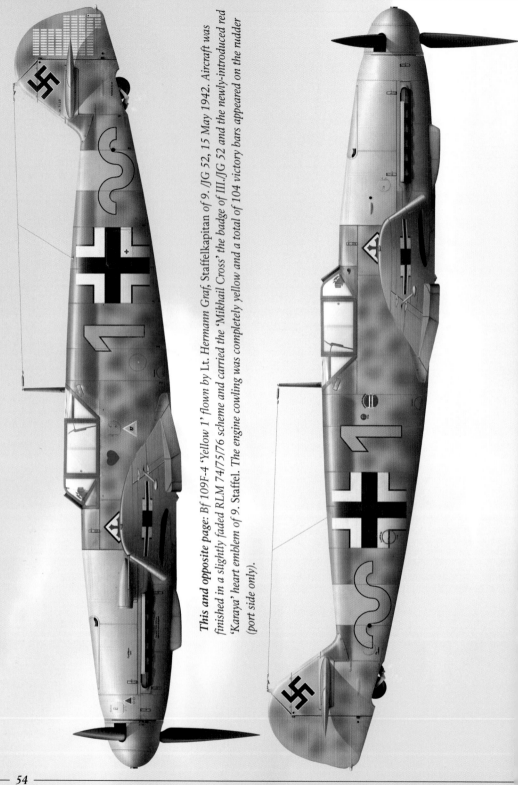

This and opposite page: Bf 109F-4 'Yellow 1' flown by Lt. Hermann Graf, Staffelkapitan of 9. /JG 52, 15 May 1942. Aircraft was finished in a slightly faded RLM 74/75/76 scheme and carried the 'Mikhail Cross' the badge of III./JG 52 and the newly-introduced red 'Karaya' heart emblem of 9. Staffel. The engine cowling was completely yellow and a total of 104 victory bars appeared on the rudder (port side only).

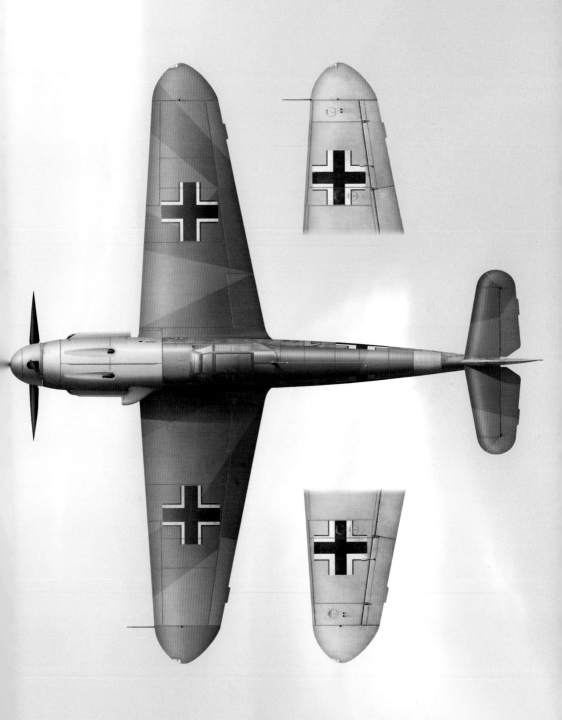

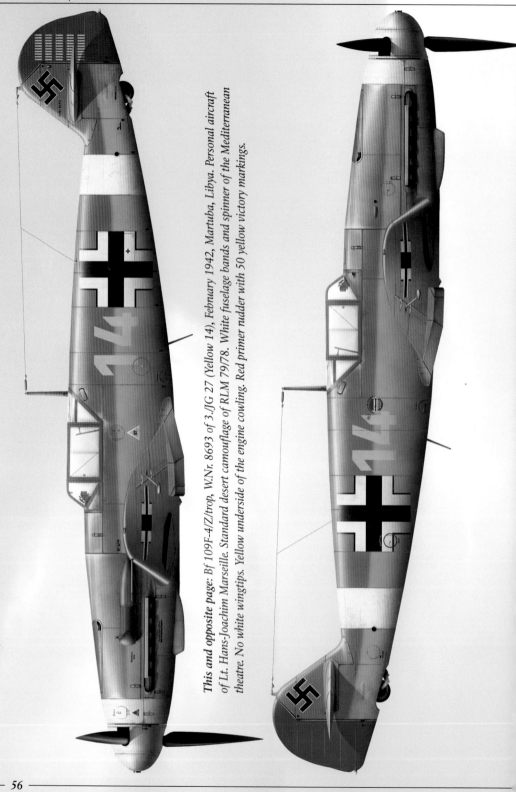

This and opposite page: Bf 109F-4/Z/trop, W.Nr. 8693 of 3./JG 27 (Yellow 14), February 1942, Martuba, Libya. Personal aircraft of Lt. Hans-Joachim Marseille. Standard desert camouflage of RLM 79/78. White fuselage bands and spinner of the Mediterranean theatre. No white wingtips. Yellow underside of the engine cowling. Red primer rudder with 50 yellow victory markings.

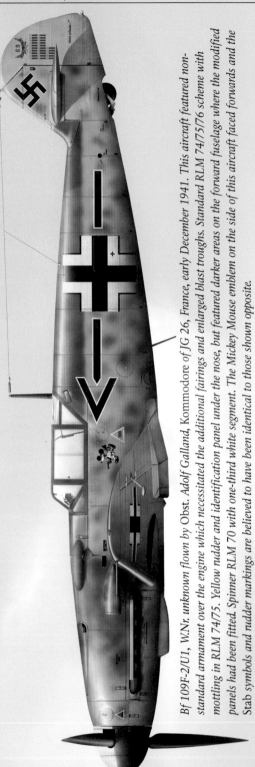

Bf 109F-2/U1, W.Nr. unknown flown by Obst. Adolf Galland, Kommodore of JG 26, France, early December 1941. This aircraft featured non-standard armament over the engine which necessitated the additional fairings and enlarged blast troughs. Standard RLM 74/75/76 scheme with mottling in RLM 74/75. Yellow rudder and identification panel under the nose, but featured darker areas on the forward fuselage where the modified panels had been fitted. Spinner RLM 70 with one-third white segment. The Mickey Mouse emblem on the side of this aircraft faced forwards and the Stab symbols and rudder markings are believed to have been identical to those shown opposite.

Bf 109F-2 W.Nr. unknown flown by Obstlt. Werner Mölders, Kommodore of JG 51, May 1941. Early RLM 02/71/65 scheme with fuselage mottle in RLM 71. Spinner RLM 70 with one-third white segment. Yellow rudder and engine cowling, Stab markings. JG 51 'Buzzard's Head' emblem on the nose.

Bf 109F-4/Z, WNr. 7308, 'Black 1', flown by Oblt. Günther Rall, Staffelkapitan of 8./JG 52, 30 August 1941. Standard scheme of RLM 74/75/76 but with fuselage completely oversprayed RLM 70 with evidence of the early scheme remained only around the swastika. Only lower part of the cowling retained in the RLM 04, also fuselage band and wingtips. The badge of 8./JG 52 appeared below the cockpit. Spinner RLM 70 without white segment.

Bf 109F-4, 'Black 5' flown by Oblt. Anton Hackl, Staffelkapitan of 5./JG 77, July 1942. Aircraft in standard RLM 74/75/76 scheme but camouflage had a slightly weathered appearance. The badge of II./JG 77 appeared below the cockpit. Rudder with 92 victory markings. Spinner RLM 70 with white and yellow portions.

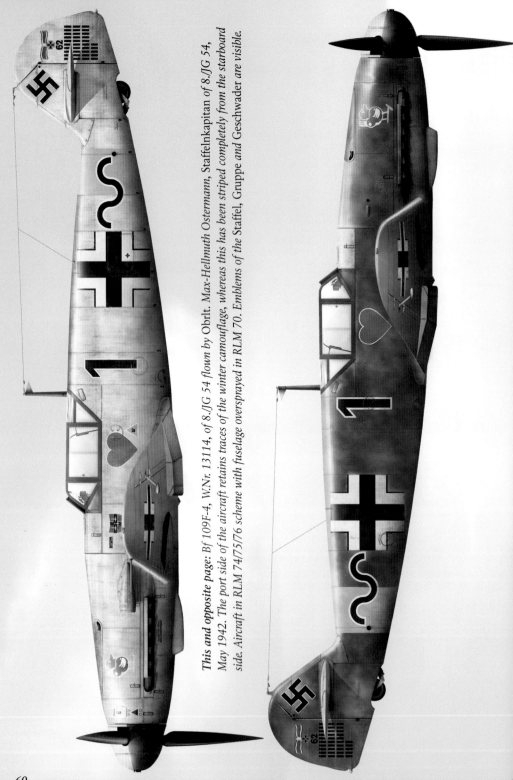

This and opposite page: Bf 109F-4, W.Nr. 13114, of 8./JG 54 flown by Obrlt. Max-Hellmuth Ostermann, Staffelnkapitan of 8./JG 54, May 1942. The port side of the aircraft retains traces of the winter camouflage, whereas this has been striped completely from the starboard side. Aircraft in RLM 74/75/76 scheme with fuselage oversprayed in RLM 70. Emblems of the Staffel, Gruppe and Geschwader are visible.

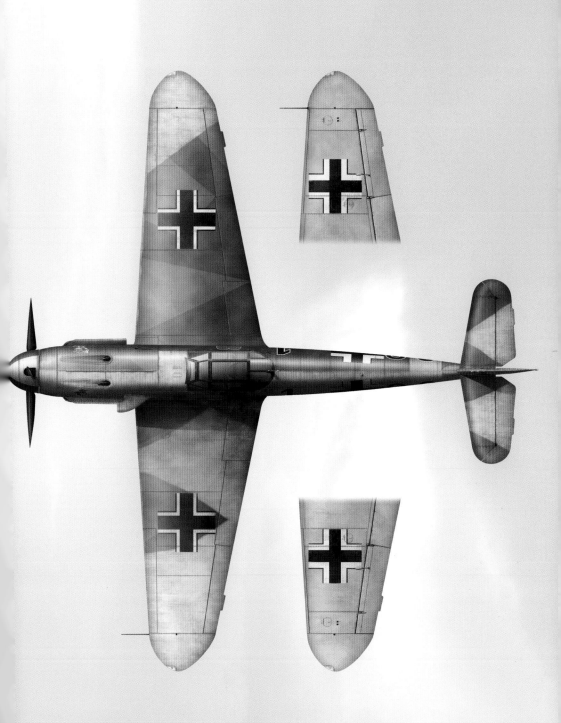

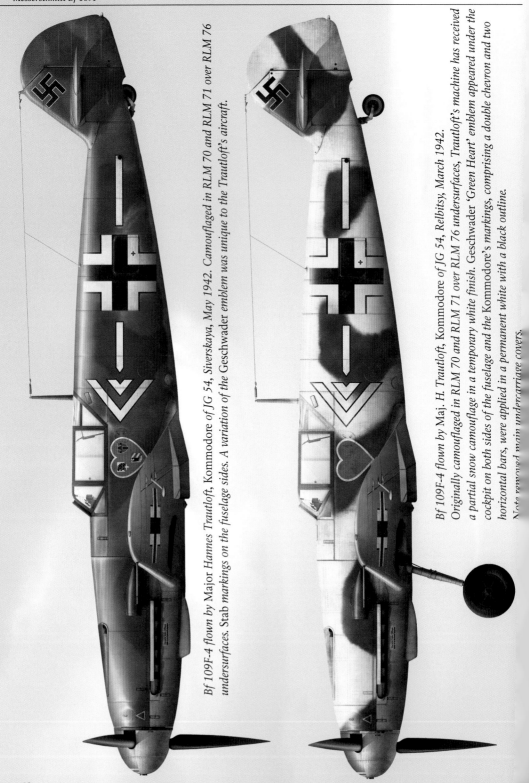

Bf 109F-4 flown by Major Hannes Trautloft, Kommodore of JG 54, Siverskaya, May 1942. Camouflaged in RLM 70 and RLM 71 over RLM 76 undersurfaces. Stab markings on the fuselage sides. A variation of the Geschwader emblem was unique to the Trautloft's aircraft.

Bf 109F-4 flown by Maj. H. Trautloft, Kommodore of JG 54, Relbitsy, March 1942. Originally camouflaged in RLM 70 and RLM 71 over RLM 76 undersurfaces, Trautloft's machine has received a partial snow camouflage in a temporary white finish. Geschwader 'Green Heart' emblem appeared under the cockpit on both sides of the fuselage and the Kommodore's markings, comprising a double chevron and two horizontal bars, were applied in a permanent white with a black outline. Note removed main undercarriage covers.

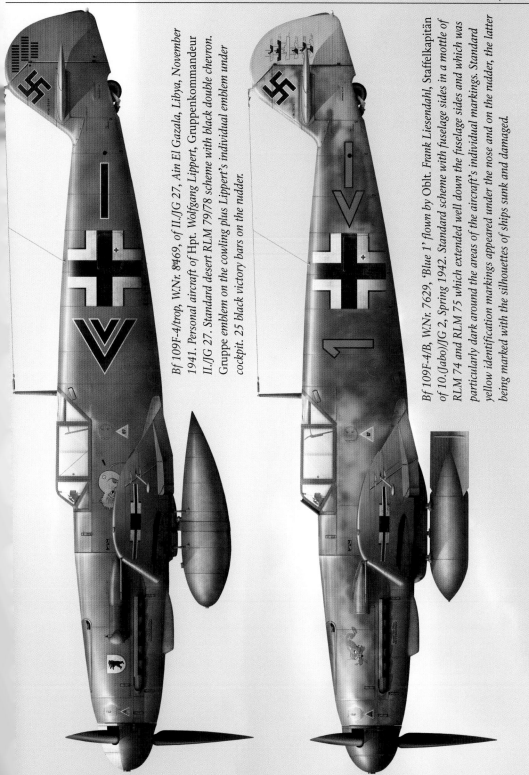

Bf 109F-4/trop, W.Nr. 8469, of II./JG 27, Ain El Gazala, Libya, November 1941. Personal aircraft of Hpt. Wolfgang Lippert, Gruppenkommandeur II./JG 27. Standard desert RLM 79/78 scheme with black double chevron. Gruppe emblem on the cowling plus Lippert's individual emblem under cockpit. 25 black victory bars on the rudder.

Bf 109F-4/B, W.Nr. 7629, 'Blue 1' flown by Oblt. Frank Liesendahl, Staffelkapitän of 10.(Jabo)/JG 2, Spring 1942. Standard scheme with fuselage sides in a mottle of RLM 74 and RLM 75 which extended well down the fuselage sides and which was particularly dark around the areas of the aircraft's individual markings. Standard yellow identification markings appeared under the nose and on the rudder, the latter being marked with the silhouettes of ships sunk and damaged.

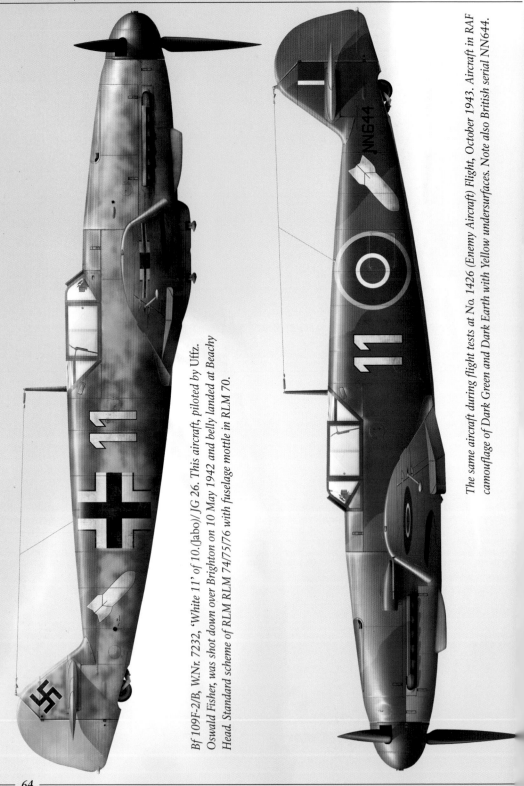

Bf 109F-2/B, WNr. 7232, 'White 11' of 10.(Jabo)/ JG 26. This aircraft, piloted by Uffz. Oswald Fisher, was shot down over Brighton on 10 May 1942 and belly landed at Beachy Head. Standard scheme of RLM RLM 74/75/76 with fuselage mottle in RLM 70.

The same aircraft during flight tests at No. 1426 (Enemy Aircraft) Flight, October 1943. Aircraft in RAF camouflage of Dark Green and Dark Earth with Yellow undersurfaces. Note also British serial NN644.

Bf 109F-2, W.Nr. 6674, flown by Hptm. Heinz Bretnütz, Kommandeur of II./JG 53. RLM 02/71/65 scheme. Entire nose painted in yellow, except for RLM 71 spinner backplate. Kommandeur insignia and unit's emblem painted on the both sides of the fuselage. Note telescope sight and the name 'Peter' painted under the cockpit. Yellow rudder with 30 red victory bars.

Bf 109F-2 used at Werneuhen Fliegerschule, 1942. Non-standard camouflage of RLM75/76 with darker patch overpainting the earlier unit markings. Spinner RLM 70 with one-third white portion.

Bf 109F-4/trop/R8, VO+SU. Reconnaissance camera window under fuselage is visible. Standard desert camouflage of RLM 79/78 with white fuselage band. Yellow lower part of the cowling. Spinner RLM 70.

Bf 109F-2, 'Black 2' of I./JG 51, April 1941. One of the early Bf 109Fs in RLM 71/02/65 scheme and very light fuselage mottle. Spinner in RLM 70 with one-third segment in white. Note unfinished unit emblem below the cockpit. Nose and rudder RLM 04.

Bf 109F-4, W.Nr. 13388, 'White 5' usually flown by Lt. Gerhard Barkhorn, Staffelkapitän of 4./JG 52, June 1942. Standard RLM 74/75/76 scheme with rather heavy mottling. Yellow nose and wingtips with rather unusual yellow fuselage band. Backhorn's wife's name, 'Christl', was painted in white below the canopy. 25 white victory bars on the rudder.

Bf 109F-4, W.Nr. 7221, 'Yellow 7' flown by Oblt. Heinrich Kraft, Staffelkapitän of 3./JG 51, Soltry, February 1942. Aircraft in temporary winter finish. The white was applied in varying densities. Darker patches – canopy framing and around the swastika and W.Nr. – were the original RLM 74/75/76 scheme. Yellow paint on the rudder is also partially visible. Yellow lower part of the cowling and wingtips. No main undercarriage covers and fixed tail wheel.

Bf 109F-4, W.Nr. 13220, 'Yellow 4', of 9./JG 3, May 1942. Personal aircraft of Ofw. Eberhard von Boremski. Aircraft originally in desert scheme of RLM 79/78 adopted to Russian conditions by adding RLM 70 and RLM 75. Tip of the spinner, lower cowling wingtips and fuselage band in yellow, RLM 04. 43 white victory bars on the rudder plus name 'Maxi' painted under the canopy.

Bf 109F-2 flown by Hptm. Hans Philipp, Grupenkommandeur of I./JG 54, Krasnogvardiesk, March 1942. Aircraft in unique JG 52 two tone green camouflage overpainted in white. Both Gruppe and Geschwader badges plus Stab markings. Rudder with 90 victories and special decorations to celebrate the Knight's Cross received after 50th victory.

Bf 109F-2 of III./JG 3, July 1942. Personal aircraft of Lt. Heinrich von Einsiedel, Technical Officer of the unit. Standard RLM 74/75/76 scheme with fuselage mottling in RLM 74 and RLM 75 softly applied. Gruppe and Geschwader emblems were painted on the both sides. White victory bars with RAF roundels and Red Stars above. Yellow fuselage bands and lower part of the cowling.

Bf 109F-2, 'Yellow 4' of 6./JG 54, July 1941. Flown by Lt. Hans Beisswenger, Staffelnkapitän of the unit. Standard scheme RLM 74/75/76 with fuselage sides overpainted in patches of RLM 02 around which lines in RLM 70 were sprayed. Spinner was half RLM 70 half white with yellow tip. Yellow fuselage band and wingtips. Gruppe emblem in front of the canopy, both sides.

This and opposite page: Bf 109F-4/R8 (Reconnaissance version of F-4), code F6+TH of 1. Staffel (F)/122 (Long range Reconnaissance Group) in Italy. Aircraft has one aerial camera mounted in the fuselage. The sawtooth edge paint scheme (RLM 74/75/76 with heavy mottling) on the upper wings is typical for many aircraft assigned to reconnaissance units. White fuselage band and unit emblem on both sides.

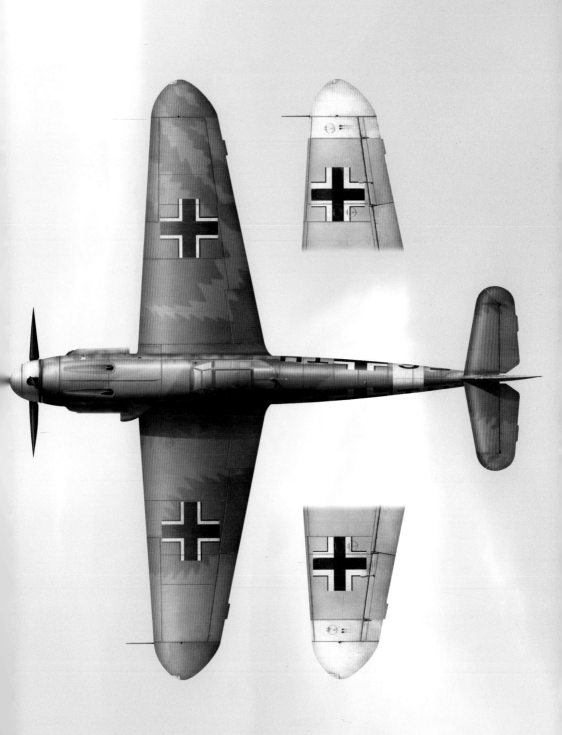

Bf 109F-4, W.Nr. 8334, 'White 1' flown by Oblt. Wolfdieter Huy, Staffelkapitan of 7./JG 77, July 1941. Aircraft was resprayed with RLM 70, the lower fuselage sides being further darkened by exhaust deposits. The rudder decoration shown here is just one of several variations seen on aircraft flown by this pilot. Yellow fuselage band. Unit emblem on both sides of the fuselage.

Above and opposite page: Bf 109F-2, W.Nr. 8085 flown by Lt. Jürgen Harder of Stab III./JG 53, Summer 1941. Aircraft in standard RLM 74/75/76 scheme but with any RLM 02 and RLM 70 mottling being confined to the rudder area and the yellow nose. Interesting is the port wing uppersurfaces, which appear to be in a single colour, and the unusual Stab markings. Yellow fuselage band. Unit emblem on the nose and white name 'Harro' under the cockpit. Spinner RLM 70 with yellow tip also oversprayed in green.

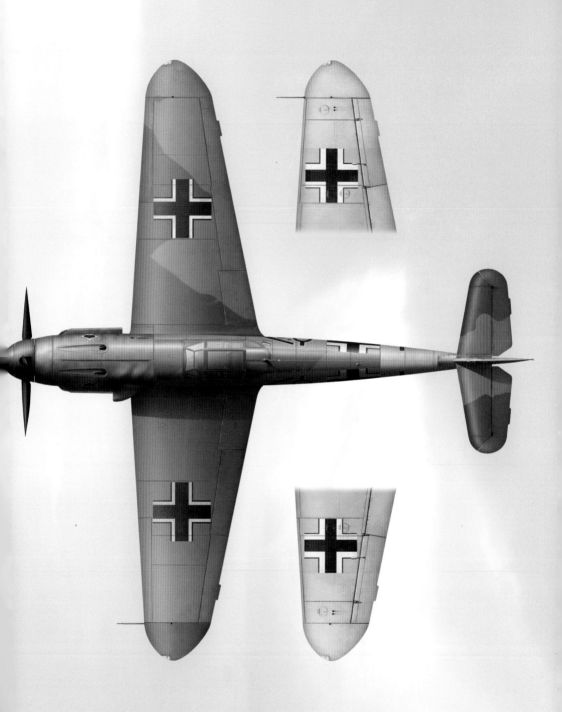

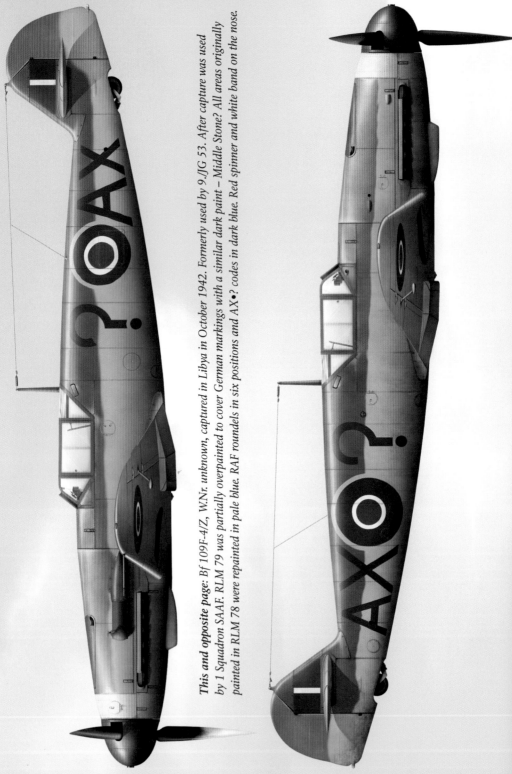

This and opposite page: Bf 109F-4/Z, W.Nr. unknown, captured in Libya in October 1942. Formerly used by 9./JG 53. After capture was used by 1 Squadron SAAF. RLM 79 was partially overpainted to cover German markings with a similar dark paint – Middle Stone? All areas originally painted in RLM 78 were repainted in pale blue. RAF roundels in six positions and AX•? codes in dark blue. Red spinner and white band on the nose.

Originally Bf 109F-4, WNr. 7640, captured in Russia on 29 May 1942 and later sent to USA for evaluations. In USA received number EB-1 (Engineering Branch-1). Aircraft painted in Olive Drab and Neutral Grey with American national insignia in four positions.

In the photo: After organization changes in 1943 markings were changed to EB-100 (Evaluation Branch-100). Also aircraft received the new US insignia with bars. (US National Archives)

Bf 109F-4, V039, pilot Őrnagy Aladár Heppes, 5/I. vadászosztály törzs, Kharkov airfield, 30 May 1943. Scheme RLM 74/74/76. Yellow Axis Eastern Front theatre marking in RLM 04, or RLM 27. Hungarian national colours Red, White and Green. RLM 70 spinner. 'Red Puma' squadron emblem. Note that this 'Friedrich' was fitted with the engine cowling of the later 'Gustav' model, identifiable by the two small air inlets on the front area. (photo György Punka coll. via Dénes Bernád)

Detail Photos
General View

Bf 109F-2 from I./JG 51 from the summer of 1941. The rear view mirror fitted in the windscreen can be seen clearly, many of these having been fitted in Jagdwaffe units in the summer and autumn of 1941.
(MT via M. Krzyżan)

Bf 109F-2s from Stab./JG 2 in Northern France, 1941. Both wings that had fought against the RAF, JG 2 and JG 26, had re-equipped completely with the new variant of the Bf 109 by the spring of that year. (B. Barbas)

Above: Bf 109F of I./JG 54 during fighting against the USSR in the second half of 1941. The photo show that the unit applied a special camouflage to its Bf 109Fs throughout the period. (Author's coll.)

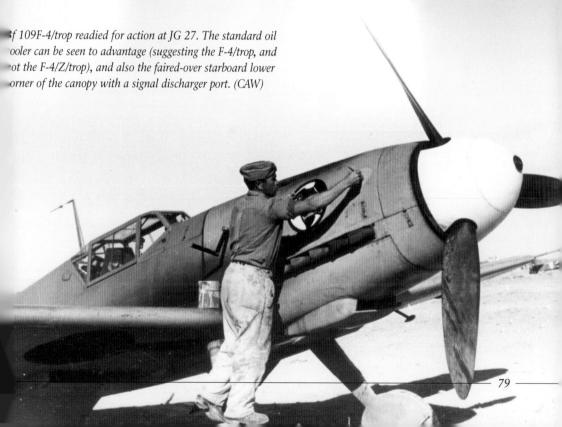

Bf 109F-4/trop readied for action at JG 27. The standard oil cooler can be seen to advantage (suggesting the F-4/trop, and not the F-4/Z/trop), and also the faired-over starboard lower corner of the canopy with a signal discharger port. (CAW)

Fuselage

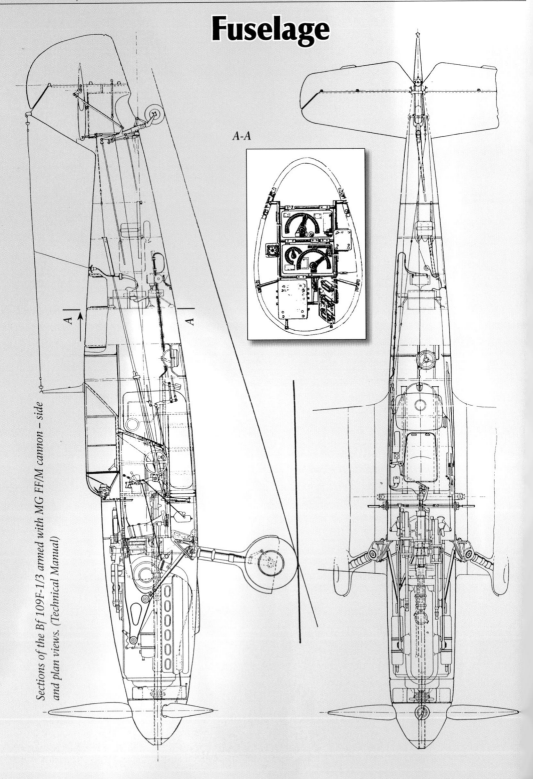

A-A

Sections of the Bf 109F-1/3 armed with MG FF/M cannon – side and plan views. (Technical Manual)

Above: Port side of the Bf 109F, 'Red 9' of 9./JG 54, winter 1942, Russia. Note fixed tail wheel. (M. Kruk)

Below: Bf 109F-4/Z, W.Nr. 10132 of 2./JG 5 flown by Hptm Horst Carganico. *Now preserved in Canadian National Air Museum, Ottawa, Canada incorporating parts from Bf 109 W.Nr. 26129. Port side of the fuselage, just behind the cockpit. (D. Allen)*

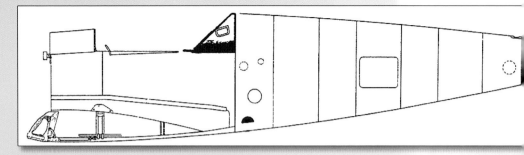

Above: *Port side of the fuselage showing fuselage sections.*

Right: *Fuselage footstep construction. (Both drawing from the Spare Parts Catalogue)*

Bottom: *Port side fuselage. Note sections numbers painted on the lower part of the fuselage. (D. Allen)*

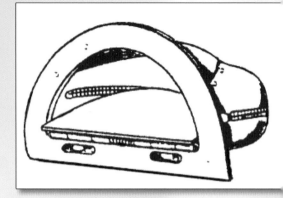

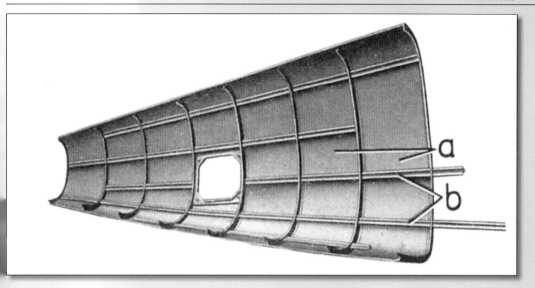

Above: Photo from the Technical Manual showing ventral construction of the fuselage.
a – port fuselage panels
b – fuselage stringer.

Below: Port side of the fuselage. Footstep, and access panels are visible. Note also aerial root at the 5th bulkhead.
(D. Allen)

Two photos of the starboard side of the fuselage just in front of the canopy. Note fasteners details.
Note that windscreen is not original.

Fastener construction. Drawing from Spare Parts Manual.

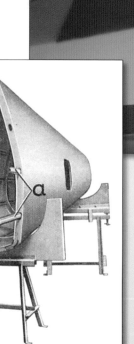

Rear part of the fuselage – construction details. Photo from the Technical Manual.

Above: Shot of a Bf 109F from Stab./JG 2, here an F-4, as shown by the marking on the fuel filler under the cockpit, indicating the requirement to use 87-octane petrol for the DB 601E engine. (B. Barbas)

Above and below: Two photos of the starboard rear fuselage. (D. Allen)

Underside of the central fuselage. Fuel tank access panel is visible (D. Allen)

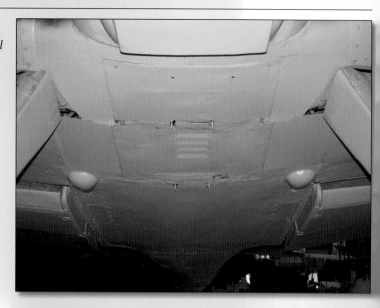

Right: *Starboard fuselage, just behind the cockpit. External power socket and the filler hatch for compressed air to load the machine guns are visible.*
(D. Allen)

Bottom: *Bf 109F flown by Oblt. Heinz Schumann Stab I./JG 51, summer 1941. Crash landed somewhere in Russia.*
(Stratus coll.)

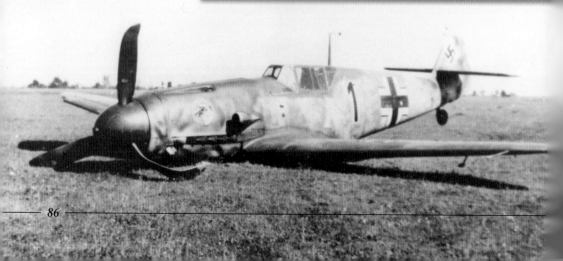

Engine

A photo depicting the ease of dismantling and servicing the DB 601/605 on the Bf 109F/G. (Author's coll.)

DB 601 engine servicing on a Bf 109F. Note open engine covers. (Stratus coll.)

Above: One of the earliest DB 601 prototype engines, which then evolved into the DB 601N and DB 601E used as power plants in the Bf 109F.

Below: Preserved DB 601 engine in Ottawa. Starboard engine mount is clearly visible. (D. Allen)

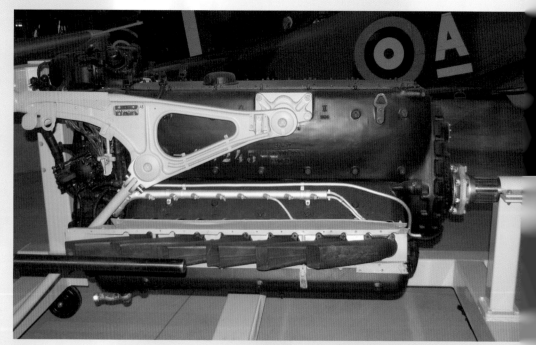

Details of the Bf 109F engine mount.

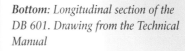

3/4 front view of the preserved DB 601 engine. (both D. Allen)

Bottom: *Longitudinal section of the DB 601. Drawing from the Technical Manual*

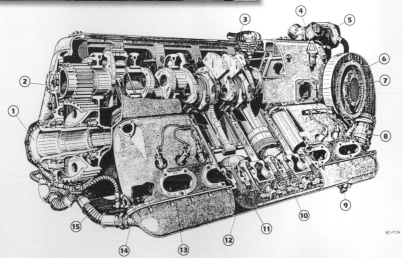

Two shots depicting the easy access to the engine thanks to the three cowling panels. (Technical Manual)
Upper photo
a. port upper engine cover
b. air intake
c. cover bracket
d, fasteners

Lower photo:
a. starboard upper engine cover
b. lower engine cover
c. starboard bracket
d. cooler flap
e. fasteners

Bottom: Port side of the DB601 engine installation. The oil cooler cannot be seen as it was fixed in the lower engine cowling.
a. fuselage regulation mounting point
b. engine mount
c. engine strut mounting point
d. supercharger air inlet
g. exhaust pipes
h. pressure-fluid tank
i. coolant tank
k. valve
o. lower engine cover
p. engine strut
q. pipe
r. clamp
s fuel hose
u. coolant pipe

Two wartime photos of the DB601 engine servicing.
Above: Bf 109F of JG 27 in Africa. (Flugzeug Publikactions GmbH).
Below: Unknow Bf 109F with upper engine covers removed. (Stratus coll.)

Above. *Engine starter.*
(Technical Manual)

Right: *Two photos of*
the engine cowling of the
Bf 109F-4/Z. Note restored
stencils. (D. Allen)

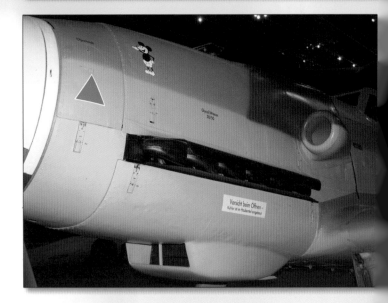

Drawing of the lower engine
cover, inside view.
(Technical Manual)

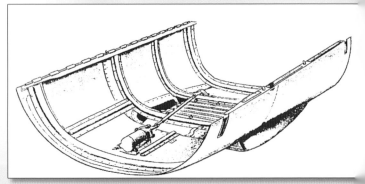

Port side of the engine cowling. Note the shape of the supercharger intake – Bf 109F-4/Z.

Below: Drawings of the front engine cowling with oil filler cap in open position. (Technical Manual)

Below: Another wartime photo of DB601 engine servicing. Details of the engine installation are visible. Note also canopy and cockpit details (Stratus coll.)

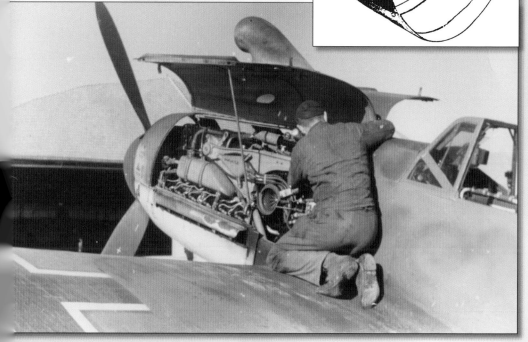

Two photos of the spinner. Unique Bf 109 spinner shape is visible.

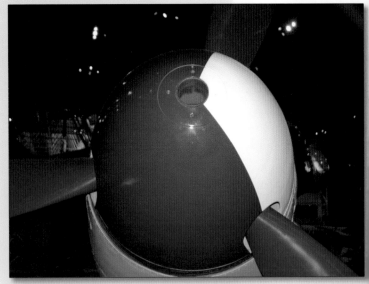

The oil cooler inlet, front view. Note that it is a deeper cooler used on Bf 109F-4/Z (all D. Allen)

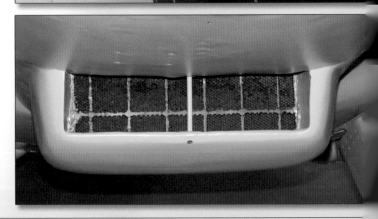

Above: *Servicing and refuelling of Bf 109F-4 of III./JG 54 during operations on the Eastern Front.*
(Flugzeug Publikations, GmbH)

Right. Fuel tank mounted behind the pilot seat.
(Technical Manual)

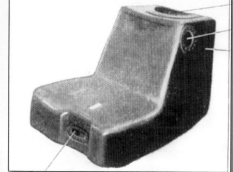

Fuel system of the Bf 109F. (Technical Manual)

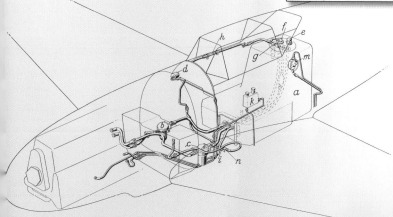

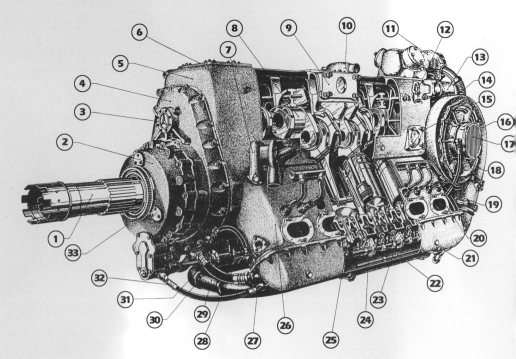

Front and rear view of the DB 601 with the crankshaft position visible. (Technical Manual)

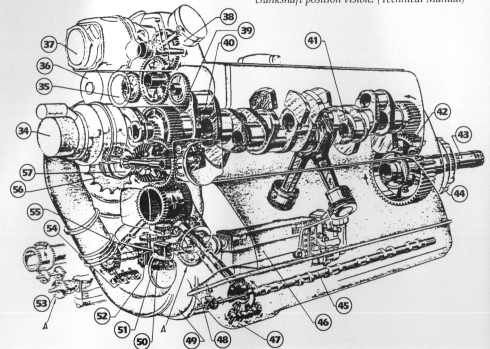

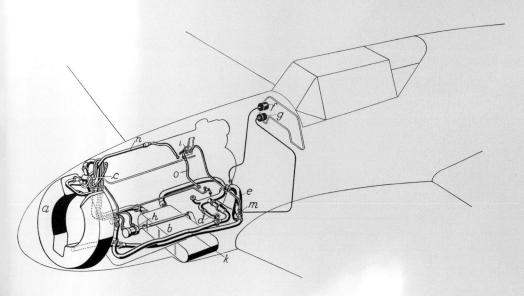

Above: Oil cooling system of the Bf 109F.

Below: Engine cooling system of the Bf 109F. (Both drawings from Technical Manual)

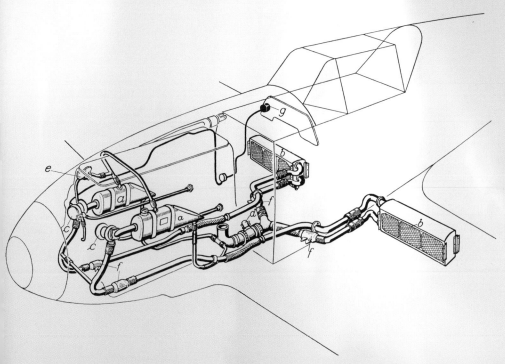

Wing

One of the first Bf 109F produced by WNF factory in a demonstration flight over the Alps, showing the beauty the Bf 109F to advantage. The photo was taken for a Messerschmitt advertisement. (Author's coll.)

Landing flap in the 'down' position. (D. Allen)

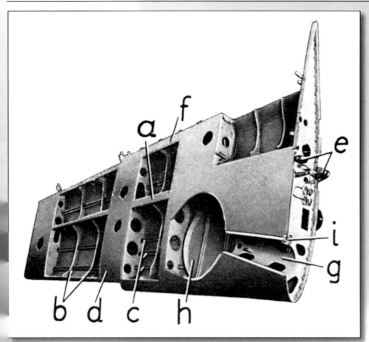

*Port wing construction.
Underside. (Technical Manual)*

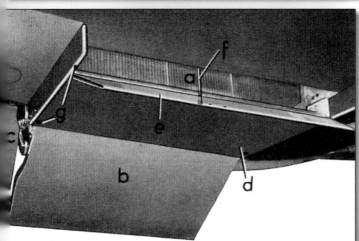

*Underwing radiator
construction.
(Technical Manual)
a. radiator
b. lower flap
c. hinge
d. radiator cover
e. inlet flap
g. support
f. push rod*

*The joint between the rounded
tip and the wing.
(Technical Manual)*

Starboard wing tip. Navigation light is clearly visible.

Starboard wing underside. Note aileron hinges and external mass balance.

Starboard radiator, side view. Note the outer rear part of the cover has been removed, (all D. Allen)

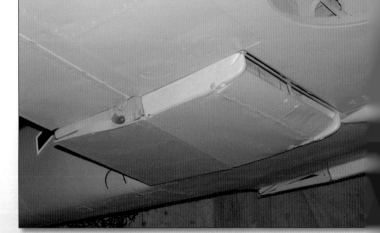

Above: Rather rare photo of the wing underside. Bf 109F-2 of 8./JG 54 ended up on its nose during winter 1941/42. (Flugzeug Publikations GmbH)
Below: Centre part of the starboard wing showing the wing radiator flaps in open (normal) position. (D. Allen)

Above, left: Port wing tip with pitot tube.

Above, right: Aileron mass balance.

Right: Fuselage-wing joint section front view.
(all D. Allen)

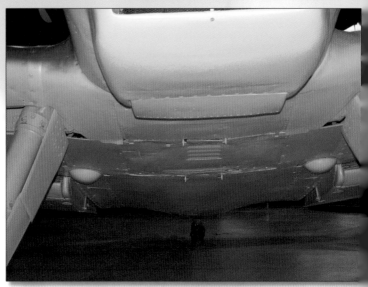

Below: Underside of the starboard wing. Damaged Bf 109F after take-off accident.
(Flugzeug Publikations GmbH)

Canopy

Above: Oberst *Werner Mölders in his Bf 109F-1. Note details of the canopy framing. (M. Kruk)*
Below: *Canopy details of the preserved Bf 109F-4. (D. Allen)*

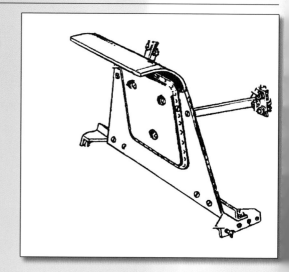

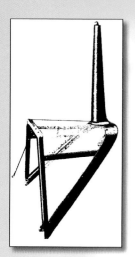

Above right: *Armoured head rest, mounted on a Bf 109F-4.*

Details of the canopy construction.

(All drawings Spare Part Manual)

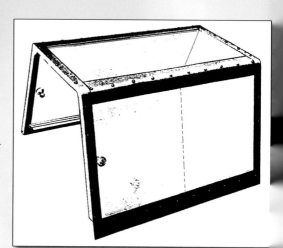

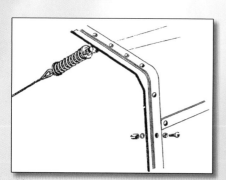

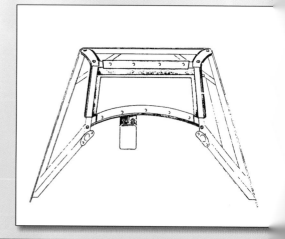

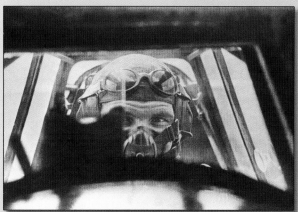

Above: Details of the port side of the
windscreen, view from the cockpit. (Technical
Manual)
Above, right: Pilot in the cockpit seen
through the windscreen. (CAW)
Right: The close-up shot of the cockpit
shows the faired-over starboard side of the
cockpit canopy with an opening for the signal
discharger, and the armoured glass panel on
the windscreen. (NASM)

*Canopy with additional armoured 57 mm glass fitted.
Hptm. Hans von Hahn, Kommandeur of 1./JG 3 in his
aircraft. See colour profile at page 53. (Stratus coll.)*

Cockpit

Bf 109F-2, W.Nr. 12764 flown by Hptm. *Rolf Pingel landed in UK. (Author's coll.)*
1. *Fuel injection pump; 2. Fuel cock lever; 3. Selector switch for the prop pitch; 4. Throttle with propeller control;*
5. Engine starting switch; 6. Switch for landing gear retraction; 7. Hand grip for spark plug cleaning; 8. Ignition
switch; 9. Propeller pitch indicator; 9. Coolant exit and oil intake temperature indicator; 11. Fuel warning lamp;
12. Fuel flow sight glass; 13. Hand grip for coolant radiator flap control.

Main instrument panel of the Bf 109F-2. (Technical Manual)

a. Chronometer
b. Oil and coolant temperature indicator
c. Propeller pitch indicator
d. Landing gear retraction switch
e. Master switch
f. Ignition switch
g. Starting switch
h. Undercarriage indicator

i. Throttle control
k. Patin repeater compass
m. Turn and bank indicator
n. Propeller control
o. Low fuel warning
q. Fuel and oil pressure gauge
p. Flight instruments
r. Emergency gear lowering handle

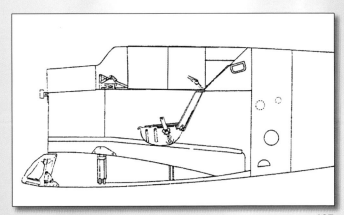

Right: Pilot's seat arrangement, side view. (Technical Manual)

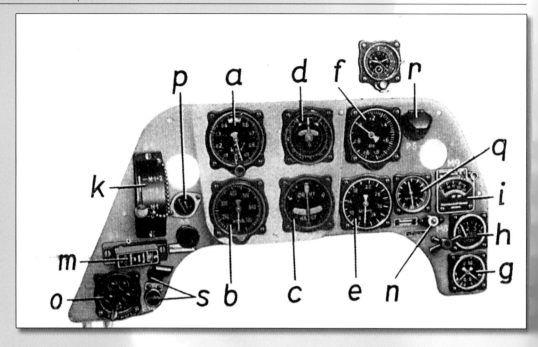

Above: *Photo from Technical Manual showing the instrument panel arrangement.*
Below: *Instrument panel colour drawing. (D. Karnas)*

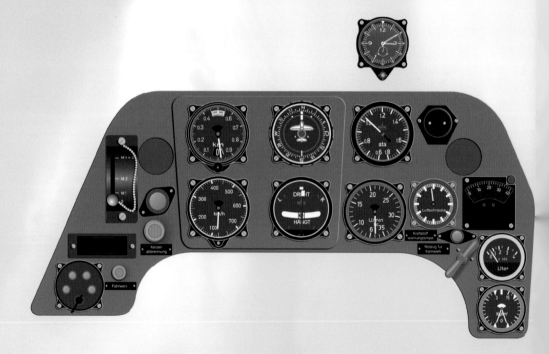

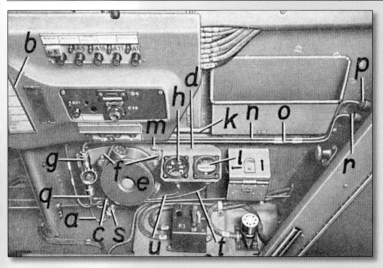

Left: *Starboard cockpit wall.*
e. Oxygen economiser
g. Oxygen remote control valve
h. Oxygen pressure gauge
l. Oxygen flow indicator

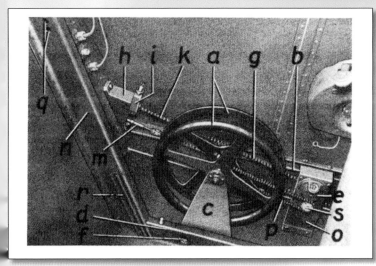

Above: *Flaps and tailplane incidence adjustments wheels.*

Left: *Port side cockpit wall.*
a. Flaps (inner) and tailplane incidence adjustment (outer) wheels.

Bottom: *Tailplane incidence adjustment control.*
(All from Technical Manual)

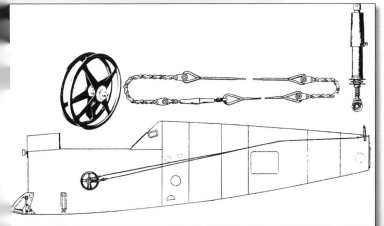

Right: *Armament controls and gun sight photo from Technical Manual.*
1. *Revi C/12 C gun sight*
2. *Gun sight mounting screw*
3. *Safety rubber block*
4. *Tinted glass plate*
5. *Reflector plate*
(…)
8. *Emergency circular sight*
9. *Power socket*
(…)
11. *Steering column KG 12A type*
12. *MG17 trigger*
13. *MG151 button*
(…)
17 *Ammunition counter*
(…)

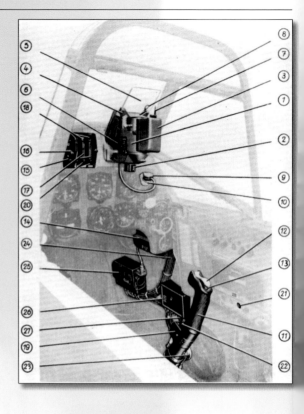

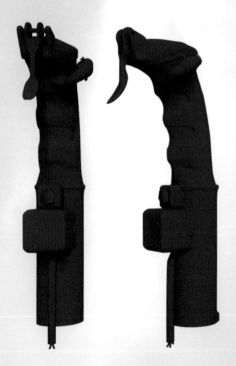

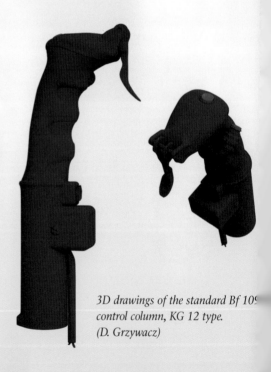

3D drawings of the standard Bf 109 control column, KG 12 type.
(D. Grzywacz)

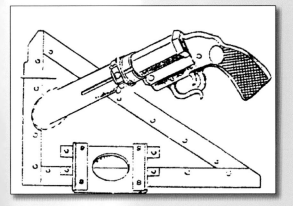

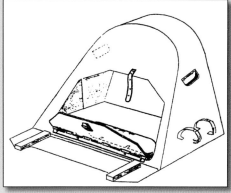

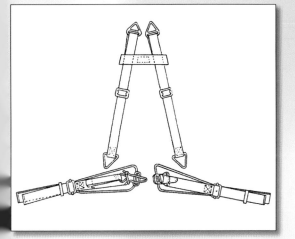

Above, left: *Signal pistol mounting.*

Above, right: *Luggage compartment behind headrest.*

Left: *Pilot's harness arrangement.*

(all drawings Spare Parts Manual)

Below: *Rear side of the instrument panel. (Technical Manual)*

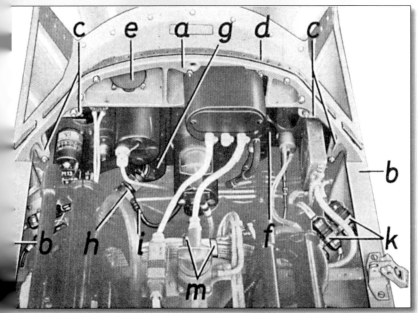

Tail

Above and right: *Port side of the rudder (fabric-covered) and tail navigation light details. (D. Allen)*

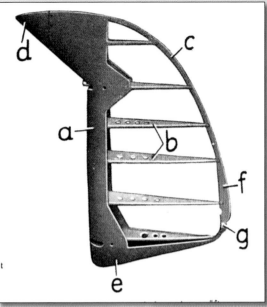

Above, left: *Tailplane of the Bf 109F-4, W.Nr. 13376 of* Stab I./JG 77 *flown by* **Major** *Heinz Bär. (AMC)*

Above, right: *Rudder construction. (Technical Manual)*

Opposite page bottom: *Starboard side of the tail. Photo taken in winter 1942. (Flugzeug Publikations GmbH).*

Bottom: *Starboard side of the Bf 109F-2 rudder. This is W.Nr. 5458 flown by* Hptm. *Hans von Hahn, of I./JG 3.*
(Stratus coll.) See also colour profile on page 53.

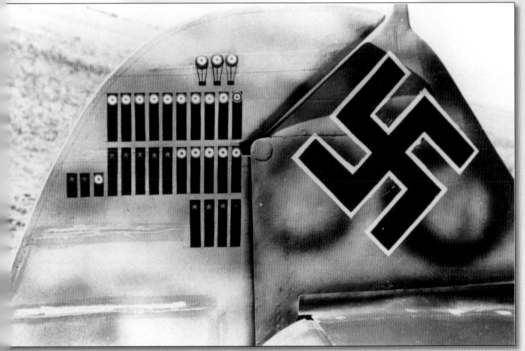

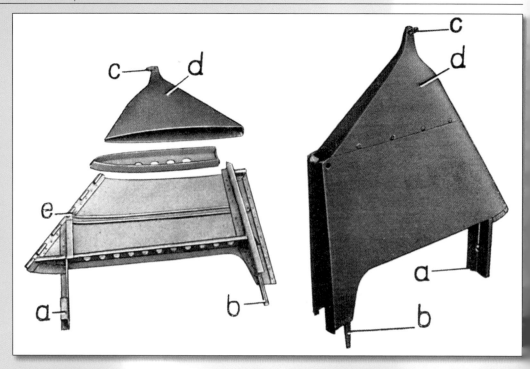

Above: Metal fin construction. *(Technical Manual)*
Below: Two photos of the fin showing details of the aerial mast. *(D. Allen)*

Above: Port side of the Bf 109F rudder. This is Bf 109F-1, W.Nr. 5628, SG+GW flown by Oberst *Werner Mölders. See also page 17. (M. Kruk)*
Below: A Bf 109F of IV./JG 52 after an emergency landing. Horizontal stabiliser details are clearly visible. Photos of the stabiliser underside are rare. (Flugzeug Publikations, GmbH)

Undercarriage

Main undercarriage arrangement shown on a wartime photo (Stratus coll.) and a preserved aircraft. (D. Allen).

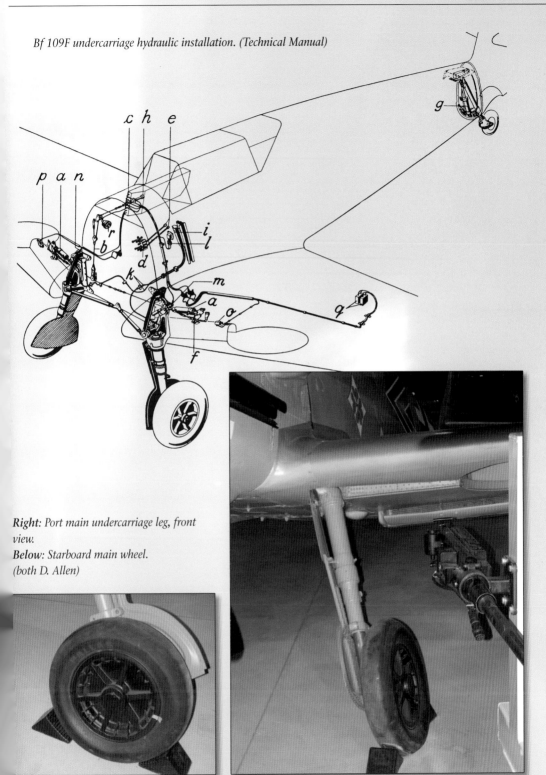

Bf 109F undercarriage hydraulic installation. (Technical Manual)

Right: *Port main undercarriage leg, front view.*
Below: *Starboard main wheel.*
(both D. Allen)

Port main undercarriage leg. Note the shape of the leg cover.

Below, right: Upper side of the undercarriage cover.

Bottom, left: Starboard main undercarriage gear. (all D. Allen)

Bottom, right: The main undercarriage gear strut retraction pivot. (Technical Manual)

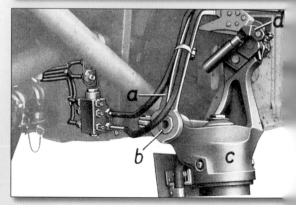

Two photos of the main wheel wells, both sides. Note inside shape and details. The wheel bay was normally sealed off by canvas cover, not seen in these photos.
(D. Allen)

Starboard undercarriage gear.
(D. Allen)

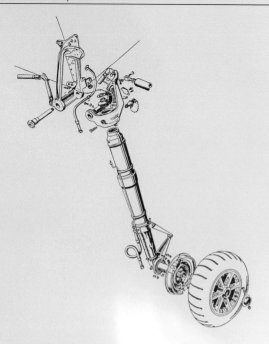

Above, left: Details of the Bf 109F main wheel leg.

Above, right. Photo of the port undercarriage leg. *(Both Technical Manual)*

Below: Bf 109F in the winter, Russia 1942. Note removed main undercarriage leg covers. It was common during snowy Russian winter. *(Stratus coll.)*

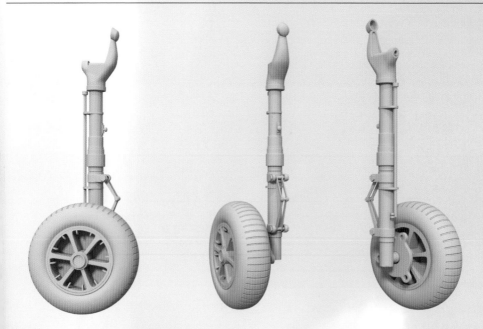

Above: *3D drawing showing the main undercarriage leg arrangement. (D. Grzywacz)*

Below: *Servicing the Bf 109F undercarriage on the Channel, 1941. (Flugzeug Publikations GmbH)*

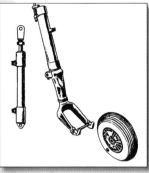

Above: Tail wheel components. (Technical Manual)

Above and right: *Two photos of the port side of the tail wheel as it is on Bf 109F-4 preserved in Ottawa. (D. Allen)*

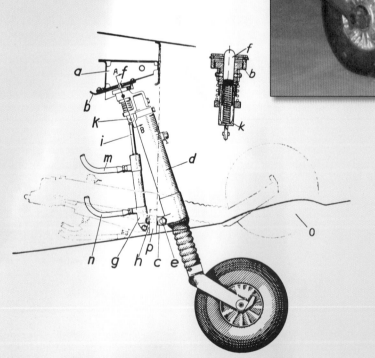

Left: Bf 109F tail wheel diagram. Initially it was retractable, but this solution was gradually abandoned.

Armament

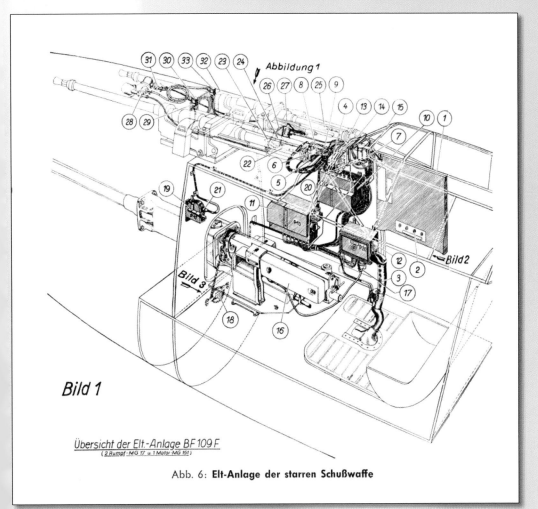

Abbildung 1

Bild 2

Bild 3

Bild 1

Übersicht der Elt.-Anlage BF 109 F
(2 Rumpf : MG 17 u. 1 Motor MG 151)

Abb. 6: **Elt-Anlage der starren Schußwaffe**

Above: *Armament installation in the Bf 109F-2. Drawing from the Technical Manual.*

Right: *MG151 removed for display from Bf 109F-4 preserved in Ottawa, Canada, starboard-rear part. (D. Allen)*

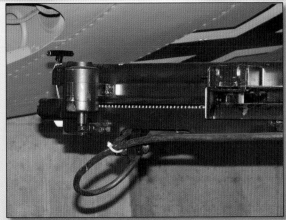

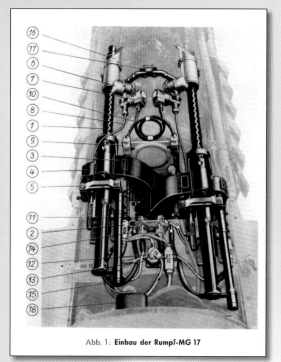

Abb. 1: **Einbau der Rumpf-MG 17**

Above: *Photo of the MG17 machine guns installation of the Bf 109F-2. (Technical Manual)*

Above, right: *Linking ammunition for the MG151 cannon. (Author's coll.)*

Right: *MG151 installation in the cockpit. (Technical Manual)*

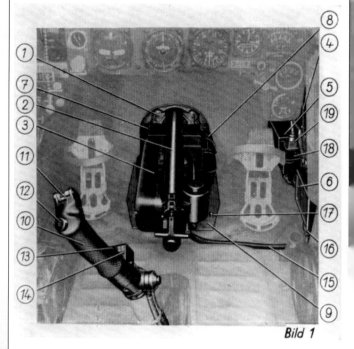

Bild 1

Abb. 2: **Einbau des MG 151**

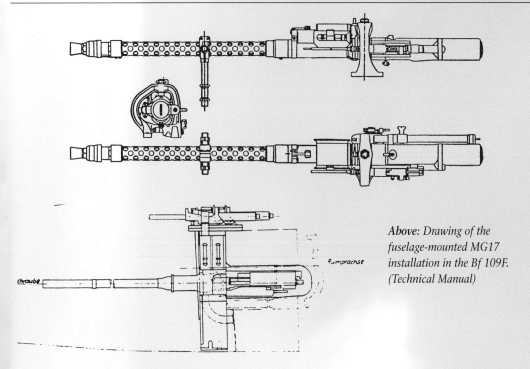

Ansicht mit MG151 Einbau (F₂ u. F₄)

Above: *Drawing of the fuselage-mounted MG17 installation in the Bf 109F. (Technical Manual)*

Above: *Drawing of the MG151 mounted in the Bf 109F-2 and F-4. (Technical Manual)*

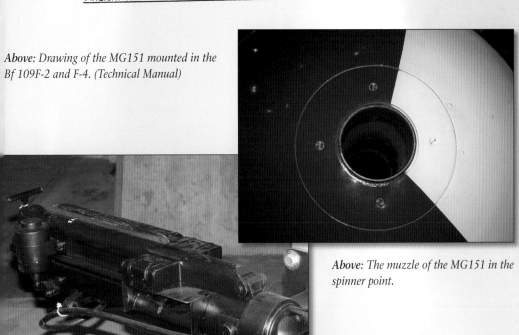

Above: *The muzzle of the MG151 in the spinner point.*

Left: *Rear part of the MG151 preserved in museum. (Both D. Allen)*

Diagram of ammunition feed for the fuselage-mounted MG17. (Technical Manual)

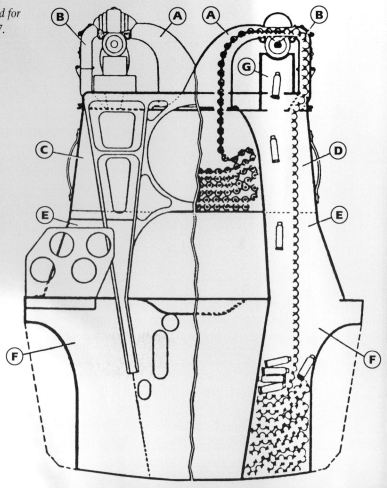

MG151 preserved in Ottawa. (D. Allen)

Above: *Bf 109F-4/B with ETC 500 IXb bomb rack and SC 250 bomb.*

Right: *Armed with four SC50 bombs, this Bf 109F-4/B belonged to 10.(Jabo)/JG 53.*

Above, left: *Fitting a cine camera in the wing equipment compartment immediately outboard of the main wheel well. The camera port window can be seen clearly in the wing leading edge. (CAW)*

Above right: *Mounting cameras in reconnaissance version of the Bf 109F. (Author's coll.)*

Right: *Arming the Bf 109F/B with two SC50 bombs. (Flugzeug Publikations GmbH)*

Bottom: *3D drawings of the SC500 and SC250 bombs. (D. Grzywacz)*